ENDORSEMENTS

The Divinity Code to Understanding Angels by Adam F. Thompson and Adrian Beale is a very insightful and revelatory read. Angels are real and more than ever they are being commissioned and activated in the earth by the hand of God. As I began reading the book, I became aware of increased angelic activity around me and the tangible presence of God increased. I pray you will experience the same!

PATRICIA KING
Minister, author, television host
www.patriciaking.com

This is one of the most interesting books I have seen in a long time. I discovered no less than 56 points worth underlining and highlighting. Here are five that stand out:

- When angels appear in a dream, vision, or trance, you will receive an authority to decree what they are relaying from God.

- In the book of Zechariah 4:1, the prophet encountered an "awakening angel."

- Angels are assigned to go ahead of you to prosper you and often act as a vanguard to disrupt the plans of the enemy.

- When people talk about angelic encounters, there is often a sense of the realm of glory.

- These types of gems are throughout the manuscript, including this quote: "There are times to share openly and times to keep silent about angelic interventions."

I will stop with the last point and suggest that if you are hungry for the supernatural realm—this book is for you!

LANCE WALLNAU
Founder, Lance Learning Group
LanceWallnauMinistries.com

After reading this compelling and timely book, you will never again have to be reminded that there are more with us than there are against us. A fascinating and enlightening read.

RAY HUGHES
Selahministries.com

My friends Adam F. Thompson and Adrian Beale have done it again! They have written another outstanding book that will help God's people move forward in their kingdom assignments. *The Divinity Code to Understanding Angels* will become an essential part of your supernatural library because the present-day ministry of angels is an essential part of God's plan. Not too long ago the Spirit had me release a prophetic word in Jerusalem. He said "I am releasing and dispatching My angels over your life right now. Some of you have been praying and praying and praying, but you must know that I have heard your prayers. They have not fallen on deaf ears, for I AM the Lord that hears you. I have heard My Word on the lips of My people and I am responding to your prayers in this day." This anointed book will assist you in connecting with what God is doing in the earth today! Angels are moving...angels are active...angels are ready to help you now. Read this book, read it again and carry it as a reference guide for angelic ministry.

JOSHUA MILLS
Speaker and bestselling author of
Seeing Angels and *Encountering Your Angels*

The more we learn and understand about God's holy angels, the more we will effectively partner with these heavenly beings.

Adam F. Thompson and Adrian Beale, in their book *The Divinity Code to Understanding Angels*, provide both a biblical understanding for angels as well as many useful illustrations to describe how they operate. Read this book and learn from two powerful leaders in the supernatural.

JENNIFER EIVAZ
Founder, Harvest Ministries International
Author, *Prophetic Secrets* and *Glory Carriers*
Jennifereivaz.com

The Divinity Code to Understanding Angels is a rich resource for this new era. My friends Adam F. Thompson and Adrian Beale lead the reader on a journey of understanding and discovery of the role of the angelic in the earth and in the lives of believers through the Word of God and practical examples. This book will assist you on your journey. May the Holy Spirit open your eyes to the supernatural realm and the angelic in greater ways as you dive into this book.

LANA VAWSER
Prophetic voice, itinerant speaker
Author, *The Prophetic Voice of God*
Lanavawser.com

The Divinity Code to Understanding Angels is a brilliant book on the ministry of angels in the earth today. Saturated with Scripture, truth, and revelation, Adam F. Thompson and Adrian Beale give clear and deep understanding into how these spiritual ministers operate in, through, and around the lives of believers. Their personal experience gives great illustration of what we see in Scripture. You will be intrigued, instructed, and inspired as you read this book. I personally loved the chapter on discernment! Not everything you feel is you. As we mature and grow in our understanding of the spiritual realm, we will have greater power and authority to help others. It's a brilliant and insightful read.

MATT SORGER
Matt Sorger Ministries
Prophetic healing minister, author, TV host
Founder of Rescuel
Mattsorger.com

The Divinity Code to Understanding Angels will create a hunger in your life for the supernatural and faith to see angels working on your behalf. As you read you will start to sense the tangible glory of God filling you with faith to partner with the unseen.

PROPHET CHARLIE SHAMP
President and cofounder
Destiny Encounters International
destinyencounters.com
Author, *Mystical Prayer, Translation to Transformation,*
and *Angels: A Biblical School of Living Light*

Adam and Adrian have done it again! *The Divinity Code to Understanding Angels* is destined to be another must-have book in any Christian library. This book provides such fascinating and helpful insights into angels and their involvement in our lives and gives answers to some of the most asked questions and misunderstandings about angels. I have such respect for both Adam and Adrian and highly recommend this book as a clear and excellent guide to understanding the function of the angelic realm.

KATHERINE RUONALA
Senior Leader, Glory City Church, Brisbane
Author, *Living in the Miraculous, Wilderness to Wonders,*
Life with the Holy Spirit, Speak Life,
and *Supernatural Freedom*

THE DIVINITY CODE

TO UNDERSTANDING

ANGELS

OTHER DESTINY IMAGE BOOKS BY
ADAM F. THOMPSON AND ADRIAN BEALE

BOOKS BY ADAM F. THOMPSON

*The Supernatural Man: Learn to Walk in
Revelatory Realms of Heaven*

*The Divinity Code to Understanding Your Dreams
and Visions* (with Adrian Beale)

*God's Prophetic Symbolism in Everyday Life: The Divinity
Code to Hearing God's Voice Through Natural Events
and Divine Occurrences* (with Adrian Beale)

*A Practical Guide to Decoding Your Dreams and Visions: Unlocking
What God Is Saying While You Sleep* (with Adrian Beale)

From Heaven to Earth: Living Life as a Spiritual Highlander

BOOKS BY ADRIAN BEALE

*The Divinity Code to Understanding Your Dreams
and Visions* (with Adam F. Thompson)

*God's Prophetic Symbolism in Everyday Life: The Divinity
Code to Hearing God's Voice Through Natural Events and
Divine Occurrences* (with Adam F. Thompson)

*A Practical Guide to Decoding Your Dreams and Visions: Unlocking
What God Is Saying While You Sleep* (with Adam F. Thompson)

The Mystic Awakening

The Lost Kingdom

Kingdom Mysteries Hidden in Plain Sight

THE DIVINITY CODE

TO UNDERSTANDING

ANGELS

AN A TO Z GUIDE TO GOD'S ANGELIC HOST

ADAM F. THOMPSON AND ADRIAN BEALE

DESTINY IMAGE® PUBLISHERS, INC.
P.O. Box 310, Shippensburg, PA 17257-0310
"Promoting Inspired Lives."

This book and all other Destiny Image and Destiny Image Fiction books are available at Christian bookstores and distributors worldwide.

Cover design by Eileen Rockwell
Interior design by Terry Clifton

For more information on foreign distributors, call 717-532-3040.
Reach us on the Internet: www.destinyimage.com.

ISBN 13 TP: 978-0-7684-5419-2
ISBN 13 eBook: 978-0-7684-5420-8
ISBN 13 HC: 978-0-7684-5422-2

For Worldwide Distribution, Printed in the U.S.A.
1 2 3 4 5 6 7 8 / 24 23 22 21 20

CONTENTS

CHAPTER 1

ANGELS GO BEFORE YOU

Adrian Beale

Unseen Servants

It is important to recognize that not all angelic activity is obvious or openly seen. You may not know angels are at work. Joshua's prior encounter with the captain of the Lord's host tells us angels were involved in the toppling of Jericho's walls, though they were not specifically mentioned at its fall (see Joshua 5:13-14 and Joshua 6). Similarly, despite understanding and acknowledging their ministry, the angels remained veiled when the centurion sought Jesus for the healing of his servant (see Matthew 8:5-13). This tells us that just because you don't see an angel doesn't mean they aren't involved.

Angels are servants of God. Proficient servants do their jobs and don't draw attention to themselves. They are at best unseen. This is especially true of angels, who throughout Scripture defer any homage given them to God. However, there may be a witness or evidence of their work for <u>those who have eyes to see</u>. (*Clear-seeing*) *- Clairvoyant*

The dictionary at the back of this book will assist you in identifying some of the physical manifestations, associations, and meanings that may accompany angelic activity. Having said that, we are not to boast about, pursue, worship, or pray to angels. Their activity is directed by God in administering the Kingdom in cooperation with people who understand their identity and mission. What is our mission you ask? Our mission is to expand God's Kingdom, bringing many sons and daughters back to the Father, and to see heaven come to earth by administering and demonstrating the promises of His Kingdom.

Angels Go Before You

Behold, I send an Angel before you to keep you in the way and to bring you into the place which I have prepared. I will send My fear before you, I will cause

confusion among all the people to whom you come,
and will make all your enemies turn their backs to you
(Exodus 23:20,27).

When Israel left Egypt, God promised His chosen people that He would send His angel ahead of them. The result of which would be the permeation of fear through their enemies' ranks. While the children of Israel saw the fulfillment of this promise more than once in the Old Testament (Judges 4:14-16; 2 Samuel 5:24-25; 2 Kings 7:6,15), God continues to go before His sons and daughters today.

The Six-Day War

In 1967, nineteen years after the reestablishment of Israel as a nation, Israel again faced annihilation. At that time, four Arab nations surrounding it vowed to militarily obliterate the juvenile nation. With planes, soldiers, and heavy armored vehicles that far outnumbered their Jewish counterparts, poised for invasion, the table seemed set for another holocaust. However, Israel's forces took the initiative and set out toward enemy lines. After being initially met with resistance, Israel's forces continued to advance into enemy territory only to repeatedly be met with inexplicable troop surrenders and abandoned tanks and heavy artillery.

Like the Syrians in Elisha's day, Egyptian commanders reported hearing the advance of superior numbers of troops in the night; and in fear of being attacked, they abandoned their equipment in order to escape (2 Kings 7:6). Israel acquired so many abandoned Egyptian tanks and armored vehicles that after the war they had enough equipment for five new brigades. So inexplicable was Israel's victory in six days that one war correspondent who covered the blow-by-blow accounts wrote, "Even a non-religious person must admit this war was fought with help from heaven." While another reporter wrote, "No military logic or natural cause can explain this monumental occurrence."

When I was pastoring, I personally experienced times when angels were sent before me to quell potential hostile domestic situations by bringing confusion into enemy ranks. One time, when I was traveling for an extended period of ministry, I prayed for angelic assistance and witnessed border security guards being momentarily distracted and deafened to my declaration at a point of entry. On yet another occasion, there was a complete turn-around in my personal finances because of an understanding and empowerment of angels sent ahead to secure and shield my future income. In opening this latter incident, let us first consider its biblical foundation.

Abraham's Servant

When Abraham's servant, Eliezer, was sent to bring a bride back to Canaan for his son, Isaac, he recounted his master's promise of an angel being sent with him to prosper his way,

> *But he said to me, "The Lord, before whom I walk, will send His angel with you and prosper your way; and you shall take a wife for my son from my family and from my father's house"* (Genesis 24:40).

To fully recognize the relevance this verse holds and appropriate it to ourselves, it needs to be noted that the servant is unnamed in this chapter. Thankfully he had been identified earlier as Eliezer of Damascus (Genesis 15:2). Eliezer means helper. Having left his master Abraham (whose name means Father of many nations), Eliezer journeys on his quest to bring back a bride for his master's son from an uncircumcised family. Rebekah remarkably left her family and returned with the servant to meet a groom she has never seen. She does so on the basis of the servant's testimony, or witness, and a display of gifts.

It should be noted that the servant left his master, taking along with him a caravan of ten camels. If he were to ride on one, it would leave nine to offer as gifts. Joining the dots we readily recognize this incident prefigures the Holy Spirit's quest to woo a Gentile bride for Jesus from every nation on the basis of His testimony and a display of the nine gifts of the Spirit (see 1 Corinthians 12:7-11). More to the point is the fact that the Holy Spirit is not alone in His quest, as there are unseen angels sent forth for the *"heirs of salvation"* (Hebrews 1:14). Thus the writer to the Hebrews is likely drawing from this episode when he writes, *"Are they not all ministering spirits, sent forth to minister for them who shall be heirs of salvation?"* (Hebrews 1:14 KJV).

Not only is this a powerful reminder to believe for a display of the nine gifts of the Spirit as we share our testimony in Christ, it also reveals and confirms that there are coworkers in the unseen realm sent before us. Angels are working with you if you are about your Father's business.

Abraham's servant was assured an angel would *prosper* his way. The Hebrew word "prosper" (צָלַח *ṣālaḥ*, צָלֵחַ *ṣālēaḥ*) is a homograph (a word with more than one meaning). It first means to prosper, to succeed, to be victorious. This is both being successful in an endeavor and prosperous in riches. Thus God caused Solomon to prosper (1 Chronicles 29:23); and when addressing Jerusalem through the prophet Ezekiel, God said,

> *Thus you were adorned with gold and silver, and your clothing was of fine linen, silk, and embroidered cloth. You ate pastry of fine flour, honey, and oil. You were exceeding beautiful, and succeeded to royalty* (Ezekiel 16:13).

Second, the King James Version of this verse concludes with *"didst prosper into a kingdom."* The word "prosper" also carries the meaning of breakthrough, to rush, and to come mightily upon. Therefore, the angel that causes you to prosper is also an angel of breakthrough.

Hindering the Angel of Prosperity

If we walk in God's ways and set ourselves to do the work that God has for us, there is still one main area that commonly hinders positive angelic activity and any breakthrough in prosperity. Adam and I learned this lesson the hard way. One time we were so busy traveling that we forgot to tithe. We continued to minister, but all of our income and even provision for our accommodation was being halved. Without discussion with our hosts on that tour, we were automatically given only one room to share. Don't get me wrong, we are not so high and mighty that we don't share rooms. The thing is, we have very different routines and we need our own space to prepare our hearts with God before we minister.

One night we were given a dream in which a bank note was torn in half after one of us had cut the serial number off the note. Cutting the serial number off indicated that the note was now unregistered. Just as it would do in the natural, this depicted that in the spirit realm the money coming in was unmarked and untraceable by God. What was happening was that the angel assigned to go before us to prosper and bring breakthrough financially was being displaced and overruled by the devourer.

Our tithes and offerings bring our finances before God and under His governmental eye and protection. By not exercising faith in God's Word, the government of hell was taking the opportunity to enforce its legal right and assigning an evil spirit (fallen angel) to steal and hamper our progress. This is highlighted in the book of Malachi, where God addresses Jerusalem and Judah by saying:

> *"...Return to Me, and I will return to You,"*
> *Says the Lord of hosts.*
> *"But you said,*
> *'In what way shall we return?'*
> *"Will a man rob God?*
> *Yet you have robbed Me!*
> *But you say,*
> *'In what way have we robbed You?'*
> *In tithes and offerings.*
> *You are cursed with a curse,*
> *For you have robbed Me,*
> *Even this whole nation.*
> *Bring all the tithes into the storehouse,*
> *That there may be food in My house,*
> *And try Me now in this,"*
> *Says the Lord of hosts,*
> *"If I will not open for you the windows of heaven*
> *And pour out for you such blessing*
> *That there will not be room enough to receive it.*
> *"And I will rebuke the devourer for your sakes,*
> *So that he will not destroy the fruit of your ground,*
> *Nor shall the vine fail to bear fruit for you in the field,"*
> *Says the Lord of hosts;*
> *"and all nations will call you blessed,*
> *For you will be a delightful land,"*
> *Says the Lord of hosts.*
> (Malachi 3:7-12)

While our natural tendency is to tighten the belt when we fear we do not have enough (Proverbs 11:24; 28:22), our tithes and offerings are a "pay-it-forward" act of faith. Though they are drawn from our past income, they send a spiritual vanguard (advanced guard) forward around future earnings.

In referencing Himself as *"the Lord of hosts"* four times in the above passage, God is revealing to us that the area of finance has eternal foundations.[1] Not only is it heavily influenced by angelic activity, but the good news is that He also wants to intervene in our favor. This means whether God reigns in this area or the devil plays havoc with our finance is really in our own hands.

Considering this passage from Malachi further, the word "curse" (רַרָא *'ārar*) is a specific verb meaning to bind (with words), hem in with obstacles and to render powerless to resist. If we or a loved one are continually being hammered financially and take a while to wake up to the fact, it is time to take a spiritual inventory and consider who we have placed in dominion over our financial destiny. God has no lack of resources and supplies; so when the passage says we have robbed God, it means we have tied His hands in His ability to prosper us by relinquishing His government over our monetary affairs.

Needless to say, when Adam and I were alerted to what was happening, we repented and we both gave substantial tithes and offerings to the work of God—and within two days, our finances did a complete turnaround.

Summary

- Though the results of their work is witnessed on earth—for those with eyes to see—as servants of God, more often than not the activity of angels is unseen.

- God sends His angels ahead of people who are about their Father's business.

- Angels are assigned to go ahead to prosper you.

- Angels act as a vanguard to disrupt the plans of the enemy and to protect your future finances.

- Neglecting to honor the work of God with tithes and offerings ties God's hands and places your future earnings outside His governmental jurisdiction.

Endnote

1. How does the number 4 relate to eternity? We live in a four-dimensional universe, which is bounded by: height, width, depth, and time. Time is the fourth dimension. Whereas we may think of time, in earthly terms, as a merely forward-marching clock, our spiritual rebirth has opened to us the eternal realm or interdimensional doors beyond chronological constraints.

CHAPTER 2

PARTNERING WITH ANGELS

Adam F. Thompson

God can speak to us through dreams and visions (for one of many examples see Genesis 41:25), but we can also partner with angels to decree what He reveals to us. When we see a natural event with a prophetic interpretation we may call in God's angelic hosts to decree and release the word of the Lord for that event.

The Eternal Family Business

Did you know that believers are heirs to the Kingdom? We are part of God's royal family because we have been adopted as His sons and daughters; and as such, we get to partake in the governing of the Kingdom on earth as it is in Heaven. We are also blessed to have the whole of Heaven backing us in our walk here on earth. While God created angels to help us and minister to us, we do well to heed Colossians 2:18-19 (NIV):

> *Do not let anyone who delights in false humility and the worship of angels disqualify you. Such a person also goes into great detail about what they have seen; they are puffed up with idle notions by their unspiritual mind. They have lost connection with the head, from whom the whole body, supported and held together by its ligaments and sinews, grows as God causes it to grow.*

Angels are servants, but they will never inherit what we will inherit as members of God's family. God—Father, Son, and Holy Spirit—not angels, is the One we seek after first and foremost.

If we imagine the Kingdom of God to be like an eternal family business, we could liken angels to being employees of the company. Picture a private organization: there is the owner or proprietor of the company, and working for the owner is the CEO. The CEO will never freely inherit the business although he may have an opportunity to buy into it. Then there is the owner's son who comes in to learn the ropes and be groomed for eventual ownership of the organization. He will freely inherit and take over the company when the time is right. We, as the heirs of God, receive free access to all of the perks from the business owner, God, because one day we will corporately own the family business.

Now, some CEOs are intimidated by this. They signed up to serve the original owner, not his son, and according to their estimation they have more knowledge and experience than the son. I believe there is a parable in this organizational structure that can be used to describe the fall of satan. Satan was delegated to a high level of management in the Kingdom of Heaven; but when the Son of God inherited the Kingdom, satan realized he would never have full control. In jealousy he rebelled, fell from his position, and was cast away.

Mobilizing Angels

As heirs to the Kingdom, believers have all the authority of the Kingdom in Christ Jesus and are seated higher than the angels. This means that believers have the authority to mobilize them as mentioned in First Corinthians 6:3: *"Do you not know that we shall judge angels? How much more, things that pertain to this life?"*

Psalm 103:20 states that angels do the bidding of the Word: *"Bless the Lord, you His angels, who excel in strength, who do His word, heeding the voice of His word."*

However, we do not exert authority over angels or even demons according to our own carnal opinions. In the King James Bible, the book of Jude 1:8 and 9 says:

> *Likewise also, these filthy dreamers defile the flesh, despise dominion, and speak evil of dignities. Yet Michael the archangel, when contending with the devil he disputed about the body of Moses, durst* [dare] *not*

bring against him a railing accusation, but said, The Lord rebuke you.

Not even the archangel Michael resorted to slanderous accusations nor spoke out of his own opinion against the devil; he used the Word of the Lord. We, too, are to use the Word of God when we mobilize angels into action, and we should never slander angels nor use them for slanderous works against others. This is true for rebuking fallen angels too. Although we call them demons, they are in fact fallen angels and as such we need to use the Word of the Lord when we rebuke them.

Angels will only respond to our decrees when we declare out of a revelatory understanding of being a son or daughter. When we walk in the fullness of God inside us, recognizing the Kingdom we have inherited, we can decree healings, deliverance, and revival. We can call upon an army of angels to go forth when we release the revelatory Word of God over the people to whom we are ministering.

Ministering Spirits

Some people freak out when I start talking about angels. They think that by talking about them I am worshipping them—but I don't worship them, I simply understand that they work alongside all of us as ministering spirits.

> *Are they not all ministering spirits, sent forth to minister for them who shall be heirs of salvation?* (Hebrews 1:14 KJV)

When your pastor is speaking from the pulpit, he is ministering to you. Do you worship him? Surely not. You don't worship your pastor, but you do receive from him because he is a minister, releasing the Word of God. Ministering spirits, or angels, exist in the unseen world, that is, the spiritual realm. When they release the Word of the

Lord, you can receive from them like you receive from your pastor. Angels will work together with you when you speak out the revelatory word released to you. Just as you would read your Bible for yourself and not just blindly follow what is being taught from the pulpit, you also would test the angels when they release words to you.

> *Beloved, believe not every spirit, but try the spirits whether they are of God: because many false prophets are gone out into the world* (1 John 4:1 KJV).

It is for this reason the Scripture exhorts us to *"Be diligent to present yourself approved to God as a workman who does not need to be ashamed, accurately handling the word of truth"* (2 Timothy 2:15 NASB).

Various Angelic Roles

There is a great gallery of angels that operate in different roles. I describe here the most commonly encountered angels that interact with us at God's command.

As mentioned in the book of Revelation, there are *revelatory angels* that bring the revelation of Jesus Christ and the spirit of prophecy. Acts 7:38,53, Galatians 3:19, and Hebrews 2:2 all refer to angels being used by God to reveal His Word. Angels also announce important messages, such as the births of John the Baptist and Jesus in Luke 1:11 and 26 and Matthew 1:20. In the Last Days, angels will be used to announce key events as mentioned in Revelation 14:6.

I have often received answers to my questions through the ministry of revelatory angels. Commissioned by the Father, their task is to bring insight when natural wisdom doesn't discern all the layers of a situation. An example of this in my own life took place in 2006, the year before Field of Dreams church was planted. For me, this was a season of fasting and intense prayer in the spirit. I was awakened from sleep to experience my spirit stepping out of my body and go from the bedroom to the living room. It was clear to me that I was not sleepwalking. I knew the difference because my then eight-year-old daughter frequently walked in her sleep at that time. My daughter would be in her body but plainly sound asleep, whereas I was wide awake yet not in my body. My attention was drawn to what I could see outside, through the double glass doors. Manifesting as a mist, like a glory cloud, I could see what seemed to be a great company of angels surrounding the house.

Then a single angel, who seemed to me to be the one in charge, appeared before me in the room and handed me a leather-bound book. The cover of the book was embossed with the word "Resolve." I opened the book and 2007 appeared at the top of the page, like a diary. There were other writings but they were all in a foreign language that I couldn't understand. Suddenly, there was an instant download of the language into my understanding and a massive impartation into my being. I received understanding of what I would be doing in 2007.

After that experience things changed. During 2007, my friend Todd Weatherly planted Field of Dreams and asked me to come onboard to assist him. I started having dramatic prophetic insight and revelation, having visions and receiving understanding for dream interpretation. This was the beginning of the flow for understanding and interpreting other people's dreams. My ability to interpret went to another level. That same angel who came to me the night my spirit left my body now stands with me as I receive visions and dream interpretations.

I don't see this angel with my natural sight; but when I sense him standing behind me, the visions come quickly. Some dreams are quite abstract, but this angel gives me insight so that I know what the Holy Spirit is saying. Sometimes the interpretation is literal;

sometimes it comes as a parable, which is when I get the personal details of people's lives—details that only the Holy Spirit could tell me. This is when He unlocks the secrets and mysteries of people's hearts.

In this highly charged atmosphere, faith manifests in response to words of knowledge and ministry is effortless. When the Spirit prompts me to give information—details about someone's child, for example: the circumstances of the birth or a particular physical condition—and God heals the person, that is when the room is primed by faith and a domino effect of miracles takes place. It's fair to say that when the angelic realm is activated, anyone can act on words of knowledge like this. The key is in knowing how to activate the angelic realm. More about that later.

I want to qualify that encounter by standing it alongside the Scriptures concerning Daniel. When Daniel had a troubling vision of the future of his people, an angel came to Daniel saying,

> *Do not be afraid, Daniel, for from the first day that you set your heart on understanding this and on humbling yourself before your God, your words were heard, and I have come in response to your words* (Daniel 10:12 NASB).

Daniel desired understanding and the angel came to give him revelation. Angels will do that: minister understanding of dreams and their interpretation. In the same way we, too, can ask the Lord to instruct ministering spirits to minister to us. The Holy Spirit is the One who gives the interpretation, but the ministering spirits equip you by bringing the atmosphere of revelation that increases insight.

There are *healing angels,* as made clear in the account of the sick man who waited by the Pool of Bethesda:

For an angel went down at a certain season into the pool, and troubled the water: whoever then first after the troubling of the water stepped in was made whole of whatever disease he had (John 5:4 KJV).

In the pre-New Testament era, people were familiar with locational portals, such as the Pool of Bethesda, where they could wait for a sign that a healing angel had ascended and descended with healing gifts. At the Pool of Bethesda, the sign was the water beginning to ripple, stirred up by the arrival of the angel. This is not a quaint folk tale—it is real. There are many of these healing angels. When I have visions about those who need healing, I immediately begin to decree the healing power of Yeshua. When I see the healing angel standing beside someone, I declare the Word of the Lord and the miraculous begins to take place.

When I am ministering, the *revelatory angels* open the eyes of my spirit so that I see visions of the healing angels standing behind people who are afflicted with disease and infirmity. Then, with the word of knowledge I can call out these people for prayer. I see this all around the world; but in this instance, I will use an example that took place in Brisbane, Australia. I was ministering with my good friend and coauthor Adrian Beale when I saw the healing angel standing in the crowded room. I called forward a woman with a word of knowledge that she had a lump in her throat. I began to decree Isaiah 53, "By Your stripes, Lord, this woman is healed! I decree for the healing angel to usher in the healing power of Yeshua!" Later, this woman testified she had been afflicted with the lump for ten years, but after prayer the lump melted away and she was completely healed. You can see her giving her testimony and glorifying God on video.[1]

There are *angels that impart physical strength*. In Daniel 10 we see how angels can strengthen a man. Daniel was overwhelmed to the point of physical weakness by the vision he had of the future of his people. When he saw the magnificent angel he declared,

> ...Oh my lord, as a result of the vision anguish has come upon me, and I have retained no strength. For how can this servant of my lord talk with you, my lord? For how can such a servant of my lord talk with such as my lord? As for me, there remains just now no strength in me, nor has any breath been left in me (Daniel 10:16-17 NASB).

Then the angelic being who, interestingly, had the appearance of a man, touched Daniel and strengthened him, saying, "'O man of high esteem, do not be afraid. Peace be with you; take courage and be courageous!' Now as soon as he spoke to me I received strength and said, 'Let my lord speak, for you have strengthened me'" (Daniel 10:16-19 NASB).

There are two recorded occasions where angels ministered strength to Jesus. The first took place during the wilderness temptation, "And He [Jesus] was there in the wilderness forty days, tempted by Satan, and was with the wild beasts; and the angels ministered to Him" (Mark 1:13).

The second occasion was in the Garden of Gethsemane, "'Father, if it is Your will, take this cup from Me; nevertheless not My will, but Yours, be done.' Then an angel appeared to Him from heaven, strengthening Him" (Luke 22:42-43).

There are *deliverance, or protective, angels*. These deliverance angels are all around us, as are all the serving beings of the heavenly realms. They are just waiting for us to activate them with God's Word. The Bible is full of Scriptures that confirm their presence. The following are two examples:

> For He shall give His angels charge over you, to keep you in all your ways. In their hands they shall bear you up, lest you dash your foot against a stone (Psalm 91:11-12).

The angel of the Lord encamps all around those who fear Him, and delivers them (Psalm 34:7).

An angel set Peter free from prison and delivered him from the hands of Herod and from the expectations of the Jewish people:

Now behold, an angel of the Lord stood by him, and a light shone in the prison; and he struck Peter on the side and raised him up, saying, "Arise quickly!" And his chains fell off his hands. Then the angel said to him, "Gird yourself and tie on your sandals"; and so he did. And he said to him, "Put on your garment and follow me." So he went out and followed him, and did not know that what was done by the angel was real, but thought he was seeing a vision. When they were past the first and the second guard posts, they came to the iron gate that leads to the city, which opened to them of its own accord; and they went out and went down one street, and immediately the angel departed from him (Acts 12:7-10).

The Bible is full of examples of these delivering angels; the following is a selection:

My God sent His angel and shut the lion's mouths, so that they have not hurt me, because I was found innocent before Him... (Daniel 6:22).

Or do you think that I cannot now pray to My Father, and He will provide Me with more than twelve legions of angels? (Matthew 26:53)

and laid their hands on the apostles and put them in the common prison. But at night an angel of the Lord opened the prison doors and brought them out, and

> *said, "Go, stand in the temple and speak to the people*
> *all the words of this life"* (Acts 5:18-20).

Several years ago while praying for a woman at Field of Dreams church, a revelatory angel gave me a vision of this woman's friend. I saw that the friend had a teenage son who was depressed and suicidal. The woman I was praying for confirmed this and became very emotional about this situation. So we prayed God's Word together, decreeing and prophesying over the boy. We called for a delivering angel to minister the delivering power of Yeshua to him. We decreed Isaiah 61 and Luke 4:18 concerning setting the captive free and binding up the brokenhearted. The angels respond at the speed of thought to the Word of the Lord, and we knew immediately that something had shifted in the spirit. Three days later the boy attempted to hang himself, but he was not successful and he suffered no significant injury. We believe a delivering angel intervened to release him from a spirit of death. All glory to God!

There are *angels that provide or bring prosperity.* Genesis 24:40 tells us the story of Abraham sending his servant out to find and bring back a bride for Isaac with these words, *"The Lord, before whom I walk, will send His angel with you and prosper your way; and you shall take a wife for my son from my family and from my father's house."*

First Kings 19:5-6 (KJV) tells of the provision of bread and water for Elijah:

> *And as he lay and slept under a juniper tree, behold,*
> *then an angel touched him, and said unto him, Arise*
> *and eat. And he looked, and, behold, there was a cake*
> *baked on the coals, and a cruse of water at his head.*
> *And he did eat and drink, and laid him down again.*

Matthew 4:11 shows that angels attended to Jesus after being tempted by satan for 40 days. Then the devil left Him, and, behold, angels came and ministered unto Him.

There are *angels that bring judgment*. Angels that bring judgment are also sometimes called *destroying angels*. Remember Sodom and Gomorrah? It only took two angels to wipe out sin and destroy a whole city:

> *When the morning dawned, the angels urged Lot to hurry, saying, "Arise, take your wife and your two daughters who are here, lest you be consumed in the punishment of the city"* (Genesis 19:15; see Genesis 19:1-25).

I'm not sure I would want those angels hanging out with me! The following are additional examples of angels bringing judgment:

> *And when the angel stretched out His hand over Jerusalem to destroy it, the Lord relented from the destruction, and said to the angel who was destroying the people, "It is enough; now restrain your hand." And the angel of the Lord was by the threshing floor of Araunah the Jebusite. Then David spoke to the Lord when he saw the angel who was striking the people, and said, "Surely I have sinned, and I have done wickedly; but these sheep, what have they done? Let Your hand, I pray, be against me and against my father's house"* (2 Samuel 24:16-17).

> *And it came to pass on a certain night that the angel of the Lord went out, and killed in the camp of the Assyrians one hundred and eighty-five thousand; and when people arose early in the morning, there were the corpses—all dead* (2 Kings 19:35 and Isaiah 37:36).

> *And God sent an angel to Jerusalem to destroy it. As he was destroying, the Lord looked and relented of the disaster, and said to the angel who was destroying, "It is enough; now restrain your hand." And the angel of the Lord stood by the threshing floor of Ornan the Jebusite* (1 Chronicles 21:15).

> *Then the Lord sent an angel who cut down every mighty man of valor, leader, and captain in the camp of the king of Assyria. So he [the king] returned shamefaced to his own land. And when he had gone into the temple of his god, some of his own offspring struck him down with the sword there* (2 Chronicles 32:21).

> *Then immediately an angel of the Lord struck him [Herod], because he did not give glory to God. And he was eaten by worms and died* (Acts 12:23).

It was an angel who brought resurrection power on the third day:

> *And behold, there was a great earthquake; for an angel of the Lord descended from heaven, and came and rolled back the stone from the door, and sat on it. His countenance was like lightning, and his clothing white as snow: And the guards shook for fear of him, and became like dead men* (Matthew 28:2-4).

This angel ushered in the *dunamis* power of God, which was witnessed as Christ was crucified and raised from the dead:

> *Then, behold, the veil of the temple was torn in two from top to bottom; and the earth quaked, and the rocks were split, and the graves were opened; and many bodies of the saints who had fallen asleep were raised; and coming out of the graves after His resurrection, they*

went into the holy city and appeared to many (Matthew 27:51-53).

(More examples may be read in Ezekiel 9:2,5,7; Matthew 13:41-42,49-50; 24:30; and Revelation 7:1-2; 8:2-13; 9:15; 15:1.)

What an intense revival these people witnessed. We are yet to see such resurrection power in this modern age.

Angels are used to *release words of encouragement.* When you speak to release the revelation of Jesus Christ and the Word of the Lord, you can be confident that the angels will activate it, or act on it. This is demonstrated in much of the Bible, including the following examples:

> *And God heard the voice of the lad. Then the angel of God called to Hagar out of heaven, and said to her, "What ails you, Hagar? Fear not, for God has heard the voice of the lad where he is. Arise, lift up the lad and hold him with your hand, for I will make him a great nation"* (Genesis 21:17-18).

> *Then behold, a hand touched me and set me trembling on my hands and knees. ...Then he said to me, "Do not be afraid, Daniel, for from the first day that you set your heart on understanding this and on humbling yourself before your God, your words were heard, and I have come in response to your words"* (Daniel 10:10,12 NASB).

> *For there stood by me this night an angel of the God to whom I belong and whom I serve, saying, "Do not be afraid, Paul; you must be brought before Caesar; and indeed God has granted you all those who sail with you"* (Acts 27:23-24).

Both the Old and New Testaments are full of examples of angels that give instruction and bring direction. The angel Gabriel was sent to tell Zacharias that a son would be born to his wife Elizabeth. This son was to be named John and was the one who would prepare the people for the coming of Messiah. And the angel said to him, *"I am Gabriel, who stands in the presence of God, and was sent to speak to you and bring you these glad tidings"* (Luke 1:19).

Then we read about the same angel, Gabriel, appearing to Mary to announce the birth and naming of Jesus:

> *Now in the sixth month the angel Gabriel was sent by God to a city of Galilee named Nazareth, to a virgin betrothed to a man whose name was Joseph, of the house of David. The virgin's name was Mary. And having come in, the angel said to her, "Rejoice, highly favored one, the Lord is with you; blessed are you among women!" But when she saw him, she was troubled at his saying, and considered what manner of greeting this was. Then the angel said to her, "Do not be afraid, Mary, for you have found favor with God. And behold, you will conceive in your womb and bring forth a Son, and shall call His name Jesus. He will be great, and will be called the Son of the Highest; and the Lord God will give Him the throne of His father David. And He will reign over the house of Jacob forever, and of His kingdom there will be no end"* (Luke 1:26-33).

An angel told Joseph to accept as from God everything that was happening to Mary:

> *But while he thought about these things, behold, an angel of the Lord appeared to him in a dream, saying, "Joseph, son of David, do not be afraid to take to you*

Mary your wife, for that which is conceived in her is of the Holy Spirit" (Matthew 1:20).

The angel also warned Joseph about Herod's plan to kill the newborns and instructed him how to protect Jesus until the danger passed:

...behold, an angel of the Lord appeared to Joseph in a dream, saying, "Arise, take the young Child and his mother, flee to Egypt and stay there until I bring you word; for Herod will seek the young Child to destroy Him" (Matthew 2:13-23).

An *angel instructed* Philip to go to a desert road south of Jerusalem for a divine encounter with the Ethiopian court official (Acts 8:26); and in Acts 10:3-22 we learn an angel instructed Cornelius the Roman centurion to seek out Peter and invite him to speak to his family and household.

In the Old Testament, the angel Gabriel was sent to Daniel to give him understanding of the visions of the ram and goat:

Then it happened, when I, Daniel, had seen the vision and was seeking the meaning, that suddenly there stood before me one having the appearance of a man. And I heard a man's voice between the banks of the Ulai, who called, and said, "Gabriel, make this man understand the vision" (Daniel 8:15-16).

And so Gabriel proceeded to explain the significance of the ram and goat in the symbolic description of latter times (Daniel 8:17-27).

An angel came to Zechariah and brought an awakening (Zechariah 4:1-2). This angel working with the Holy Spirit ushers in an awakening that primes the minds and hearts of God's people to receive eternal insight.

There are many other examples of instruction angels in the Old Testament, including those written about in Zechariah 1:8-10; 4:11-14; Daniel 7:15-16; and Job 33:22-26.

Summary

- We are heirs to the eternal family business.

- Angels are employees of the company.

- The Son is groomed to take over the business.

- In Him we are part of that corporate ownership.

- Believers mobilize angels when we decree out of revelatory understanding.

- Angels work alongside us as ministering spirits.

- Angel roles include:
  - Revelatory angels
  - Healing angels
  - Deliverance angels
  - Protective angels
  - Prosperity angels
  - Judgment/Destroying angels
  - Angels that bring instruction/direction/warning
  - An awakening angel

Endnote

1. Adam F. Thompson, Words of Knowledge, September 20, 2018; https://youtu.be/3JYC1uswFhg; accessed April 21, 2020.

CHAPTER 3

DIVINE COURIERS

Adrian Beale

Carriers of Revelation

An often forgotten and yet major role performed by angels is the carrying of revelation from the throne. Confirming this office are not only the warnings and directives given in the New Testament but also the scriptural acknowledgment of their intermediary capacity in the delivery of the law, *"Who have received the law by the disposition of angels..."* (Acts 7:53 KJV), and, *"If the word spoken by angels was steadfast..."* (Hebrews 2:2 KJV).

When we receive revelation it emboldens and strengthens us. Many times when Adam and I have been ministering, people report seeing angels speaking in our ears before we interpret dreams and speak prophetically into the lives of individuals. On one of these occasions a photographer captured on film an orb sitting directly on the top of my head as I interpreted a person's dream. This was without any evident refraction of light coming off of spotlights. Why might angels appear as orbs? An orb is circular in its outline from every direction, which depicts that it has no beginning or end and as such represents a spirit or eternal being.

It is important to note that in these situations we first pray glorifying God and then acknowledge and welcome the Holy Spirit to minister with us—and as a consequence, angels often provide insight otherwise unknown to the natural man and woman. The release of revelation increases the faith of those receiving ministry so they can receive the manifestation of what is being released. This may be healing, deliverance, conception, financial provision, direction, or a myriad of other supplies from God's Kingdom.

Angels Ascending and Descending

The Scriptures further speak of *"angels ascending and descending."* If angels are in Heaven, have you ever wondered why they first are described as *ascending*, when if they were in Heaven you would naturally think that they first descend before they ascend? The reverse is the case because they are here already in this realm and they first ascend carrying our prayers to God. They then descend with God's response to our prayers. Much of what they bring is revelation.

Manna and Revelation

Broadening our understanding of the link between revelation and angelic activity is the connection between manna and the rhema word. One verse in the book of Deuteronomy defines manna for us:

> *So He humbled you, allowed you to hunger, and fed you with manna which you did not know nor did your fathers know, that He might make you know that man shall not live by bread alone; but man lives by every word that proceeds from the mouth of the Lord* (Deuteronomy 8:3).

According to this verse, manna is what proceeds out of the mouth of God. Thus manna is recognized as a living word of revelation or a rhema word from God. Building on this understanding, Jesus spoke of having food to eat of which His disciples had no understanding:

> *But He said to them, "I have food to eat of which you do not know. Therefore the disciples said one to another, "Has anyone brought Him anything to eat?" Jesus said to them, "My food is to do the will of Him who sent Me, and to finish His work"* (John 4:32-34).

Here Jesus was making reference to revelation He had received from the Father through the agency of angels. Why would I make this assertion? This is because manna is also described as angels' food (Psalm 78:24-25), when it is likely that as spirit beings angels don't actually need to eat. This suggests that when Jesus spoke of food to eat, He was figuratively eating food in the sense that He was strengthened in hearing and delivering God's spoken word of revelation. You may have experienced this same strengthening when at a time in the natural you were personally exhausted but the moment you stepped up to minister on God's behalf, you suddenly became supernaturally energized.

Where There Is No Revelation, People Perish

So angels dispatch manna or a revelatory word from the throne of God, which in turn strengthens our faith. Do you remember what happened to the manna when the Israelites failed to eat it the same day it was collected? It bred worms, right? (See Exodus 16:20.) Worms have no backbone; having no backbone means they have no strength to stand. In essence, this demonstrates that yesterday's manna has lost the immediacy and impact to meet the cry of your heart today. This truth is both confirmed and broadened in an often misinterpreted passage of Scripture:

> *Where there is no vision, the people perish: but he that keepeth the law, happy is he* (Proverbs 29:18 KJV).

Though this verse is often the foundational leverage for many churches' "Vision Sunday" services, what it really communicates lies beyond the English translation. Here, the Hebrew word *ḥāzôn* (חָזוֹן), translated "vision" actually refers to the revelation communicated through a vision or dream. It is not so much the vision itself but the message or revelation it conveys that is the essence of this word. Thus the verse would more accurately read, *Where there is no revelation, the people perish*. The word "perish" carries the thought of letting go or loosed. Therefore, this verse takes the importance of revelation further by outlining that without revelation we have nothing in our hearts about which to build our lives and will readily fold when tested.

THE DIVINITY CODE TO UNDERSTANDING ANGELS

The secret to receiving revelation is found in the second part of this verse. It continues by stating, *"but happy is he who keeps the law"* (Proverbs 29:18). This is not a call to legalism, as it might be understood by those with an Old Testament mindset. Here the word "keeps" in context means to watch carefully over and to guard. In the light of the Cross, what we have here is the promise of the release of revelation to those who carefully watch over and meditate on God's Word. This insight also provides understanding to the source of the strength in another well-known passage of Scripture:

> *But those who wait on the Lord shall renew their strength; they shall mount up with wings like eagles, they shall run and not be weary, they shall walk and not faint* (Isaiah 40:31).

This verse adds to our understanding by revealing that interdimensional insight (revelation) is released to those who hope or entwine themselves upon and wait expectantly on God. Thus having sat with God—remembering God and His Word are one—we begin to see beyond our earthly circumstances and the revelatory food we receive strengthens our hearts and empowers us to run the race of faith and walk in love.

What Does Revelation Look Like?

Revelation is interdimensional breakthrough that may come as a series of thoughts out of the blue or as the opening of Scripture revealing another layer beyond the narrative you happen to be reading. Sometimes it is released as a dream or as the spiritual understanding of an everyday event that catches your attention. And yet, another common way in which angels communicate personal revelation is through song.

Have you ever awakened with a song in your heart that you did not go to bed singing? Very often the words of the song are God's response to the cry of your heart. Some might ask where that is in the Bible? Scripture says, *"Call to Me, and I will answer you, and show you great and mighty things, which you do not know"* (Jeremiah 33:3).

The word "answer" here is the Hebrew word *anah* (עָנָה) and has two sets of meanings. It does mean to reply or answer, but it also means to sing or shout. Thus when we ask of God, sometimes our angel may download His response encoded to our hearts in song. Pay attention to the words of that song in your heart because it may well be God's response to the cry of your heart.

Summary

- Angels are couriers of revelation.

- Revelation increases faith to receive.

- Angels ascend carrying our prayers to God.

- Angels descend with God's response.

- Manna is a parallel of revelation.

- We are strengthened in receiving revelation.

- Where there is no revelation, the people perish.

- Revelation may come as:
  - A series of thoughts out of the blue
  - Dreams or visions
  - Spiritual understanding of an everyday event
  - Songs

CHAPTER 4

THE CHAIN OF COMMAND

Adam F. Thompson

Angelic ministry in dreams and visions play a major role in the prophetic, especially when it comes to being in a position of leadership in the Body of Christ. I say this out of the experience of assisting in a church plant called Field of Dreams in South Australia in partnership with my good friend, Todd Weatherly. Receiving dreams and visions has been a great blessing to our ministry. It helped us immensely to receive guidance and warnings through dreams and visions before we had to make decisions regarding the church.

It saddens me when leaders do not recognize the potential of dreams and visions and do not accept that it is a communications vehicle from the Lord. Due to ignorance and the fear of the unknown, some leaders are quick to dismiss this and do not explore its importance in Scripture. If we understand what the Holy Spirit is saying through our dreams and visions, He can help us to build the church that God intended, and we will avoid minor glitches and major pitfalls in the process. Dreams and visions also offer insight into people's lives, showing us how to pray for them to be released from bondages and fulfill their destinies.

Angelic ministry is equally important. As ministering spirits from God, they are all around us and waiting for us to activate them. Some of them must be bored out of their minds! They are waiting for us to awaken to the revelatory understanding of what it is to decree the Word of the Lord and move into that place of authority where we can mobilize angels. It is exactly as was explained in Matthew 8:5-9:

> *Now when Jesus had entered Capernaum, a centurion came to Him, pleading with Him, saying, "Lord, my servant is lying at home paralyzed, dreadfully tormented." And Jesus said to him, "I will come and heal him." The centurion answered and said, "Lord, I am not worthy that You should come under my roof. But only speak a word, and my servant will be healed. For I also am a*

man under authority, having soldiers under me. And I say to this one, 'Go,' and he goes; and to another, 'Come,' and he comes; and to my servant, 'Do this,' and he does it."

Jesus was blown away by the centurion's faith and his understanding of the chain of command. We need to appreciate the authority that underlines God's management structure. The Scripture verses throughout this chapter prove that angels are here to help and minister to us. When we decree the Word of the Lord, angels are activated. They are God's messengers and they wait for us to call them forth to release the power of God. As sons and daughters of God, we can expect angels to respond to our declaration of the Word of the Lord. We will surely see the Kingdom of God manifest as we work together with angels to bring transformation to this world.

Frequencies in the Spirit Realm

People are very sensitive beings. It is as though we are a highway of spiritual activity between heaven and earth. This is an arena for warfare between angels and demons; but since Acts 2 when God poured out His Spirit, we have authority in Jesus Christ to exercise dominion on this highway. We are like antennas or transistor radios. Transistor radios have AM and FM frequencies that pick up the sound waves of a particular channel and allow the listener to tune in to and receive the broadcast sound. Similarly, human beings are sensitive to the frequency of the spirit realm. If we are "tuned in" to the spirit realm, we can pick up what is happening around us in our immediate environment and atmosphere. In a counterfeit way, this is how clairvoyants and those in the occult operate. Having trained themselves to be open to such things, they too pick up frequencies in the spirit realm and often see what the enemy has planned. But rather than seeing this as a warning of events that can be changed through prayer, they see it as a foregone conclusion, agree with it, and speak it into existence.

I've written in my other books[1] that there are many manifestations of the voice of God. God can speak to you in different ways. One of the manifestations of His voice is that He reveals the heavenlies to us. He removes the natural veil and opens the eyes of our understanding so we see the plans of the enemy. So warned, we are able to pray effectively into situations. I use the word "heavenlies" because it is scriptural. Others may say "second heaven," but that term does not appear in the Bible. Ephesians 6:12 says:

> *For we do not wrestle against flesh and blood, but against principalities, against powers, against the rulers of the darkness of this age, against spiritual hosts of wickedness in the heavenly places.*

The devil does not own the heavenly places. God is in full control, but He does allow certain events to happen so that we will learn how to triumph in Him. When we demonstrate that we are overcomers, we become living testimonies. God gives us the authority to take dominion over situations: to bind the workings of the enemy; to tear down strongholds; and declare the victory of the blood of Jesus and see people set free.

In James 3:5-9, the Bible warns us to be aware of the destructiveness of the tongue, *"With it we bless our God and Father, and with it we curse men, who have been made in the similitude of God"* (James 3:9).

As we bless and curse with our tongues, whatever is spoken will manifest if it is received and believed. For lack of better knowledge and judgment or a fear mentality, some prophetic people resemble clairvoyants who are in the habit of declaring the intentions of the enemy. This results in many of them cursing the people they profess to want to help. Other clairvoyants know exactly what they are doing and who they serve, and they speak out such curses with demonic and venomous intent.

I know a man who, before he became born again, went to a party that was hosting a clairvoyant. This clairvoyant, being receptive to information and visions in the heavenlies around her, moved in the realm of distorted words of knowledge. Initially, the man was not interested in her readings, but when she started speaking out facts pertaining to his life, he found himself being drawn in. She told him that she saw him losing a finger and spoke of it as an inevitable occurrence. Instead of using this vision as a simple warning, she decreed it into existence from the realm of fear. This put a curse on him. Sure enough, a few years later he lost his finger. The whole experience, based in fear as it was, resulted in considerable trauma in his life until he was eventually set free.

Ephesians 1:3 says, *"Blessed be the God and Father of our Lord Jesus Christ, who has blessed us with every spiritual blessing in the heavenly places in Christ."*

We, as born-again believers, have the sanctified spiritual gifts of First Corinthians 12 that release blessings and not curses over others. It is our inheritance to receive dreams and visions that will show us warnings in the heavenlies so that we can shut down the plans of the enemy and decree blessings. We are supposed to release blessings over others in this earthly realm.

> *And I will give you the keys of the kingdom of heaven, and whatever you bind on earth will be bound in heaven, and whatever you loose on earth will be loosed in heaven* (Matthew 16:19).

We can pick up all sorts of activity in the heavenlies; we can sense oppressive spirits, depression, lusts of the flesh, and so forth.

These are all in the atmosphere around us and do not necessarily come from our own thoughts or interactions. There may be times when we suddenly have visions or thoughts of a pornographic nature and yet we know that they are not coming out of our own being, since we had long ago brought such thoughts into submission to the mind of Christ. One of the markers that identify such thoughts as not originating from within you is that they are not accompanied by sensations of sexual arousal, either in the physical or the soul.

Immature believers, unaware of what is happening in the heavenlies, are likely to believe such images come from within. This can have people continually wondering why they have such awful thoughts and visions and send them into a merry-go-round of condemnation, repentance, and pleading for forgiveness. This is a trap of the enemy. He wants to keep us focused on ourselves so that we cannot be used by God to help others.

If you have overcome the spirit of lust, then these images and thoughts are not coming from within you. What is happening is that the Lord has removed the veil to allow you to see that there is a spirit of lust in that place. By revealing this to you, He is giving you the authority to bind those spirits and shut them down. God, by word of knowledge, will usually show you which person is being oppressed by this spirit of lust; and if you take the time to ask God what to do about it, He will give you a word of wisdom, or a strategy, to set that person free. This can happen anywhere—in business meetings, someone's home, at church—it may even be the person standing next to you in a queue. God is showing you that the person struggles with pornography and is being oppressed and bound by the spirit of lust.

Once when I was ministering to a class at a Bible college in Australia, I suddenly had flashes of pornographic visions. Through a word of knowledge and by me publicly acknowledging what I was seeing, two students later admitted they were fornicating outside of marriage. With prayer they repented and were restored to purity.

When you find yourself in this type of situation it is imperative to ask the Holy Spirit to give you the right spirit and a respectful manner of approach because the Holy Spirit is not in the business of condemning, but of convicting and restoring. John 3:17 states, *"For God did not send His Son into the world to condemn the world, but that the world through Him might be saved."*

God gives people the opportunity to repent so that they may be restored to righteousness. I believe it is very important to explore and discuss the ways God communicates with us. If He allows us to see disturbing images, we should ask Him if it is for the benefit of a person or group who need to be set free.

God may also allow disturbing images in your dreams. I was once ministering in Papua New Guinea, in the city of Lae. One night I experienced a pornographic dream. Because I was experienced in the way God speaks through dreams, I realized I was under attack. If I had not understood this, I would have awakened greatly distressed thinking that it was coming from within me. God's people need to learn how to discern whether these images come from within them as a sin issue, or from an attack in the atmosphere around them. Every individual will know whether or not he or she has an actual problem in the area of pornography.

Because the Lord delivered me from that years ago and I had been free ever since, I knew that these images were not coming from within me. I immediately asked the Lord what this dream meant. What I discerned was that something unrighteous was going on in the hotel where I was staying. I eventually found out that this particular hotel regularly rented rooms to prostitutes and their clients. I bound this lustful spirit and declared the protection of the blood of Jesus over the neighborhood. Immediately after prayer I sensed a change in the atmosphere and knew the enemy's work would not continue in that place.

Animals are very sensitive to the spirit realm, too. They pick up on spiritual frequencies. Who hasn't heard a dog whine or bark in its sleep, as though seeing or dreaming of things we can't see? I once watched a YouTube video of a dog that was lying down, fast asleep, but his legs were circling as if he was running. It seemed he was having a very fast dream! People who have witnessed such things always assume their pet is dreaming. That assumption among pet owners is quite strong, and consequently I am frequently asked if God speaks to dogs through dreams. I don't know the answer to that, although it seems reasonable to assume that He would communicate with all of His creation.

While I have never heard of any animals talking to humans to confirm or disprove that they are dreaming, Scripture records that the Lord caused a donkey to speak to Balaam:

> *Then the Lord opened the mouth of the donkey, and she said to Balaam, "What have I done to you, that you have struck me these three times?"* (Numbers 22:28)

This incident is referenced again in the New Testament:

> *They have forsaken the right way and gone astray, following the way of Balaam the son of Beor, who loved the wages of unrighteousness; but he was rebuked for his iniquity: a dumb donkey speaking with a man's voice restrained the madness of the prophet* (2 Peter 2:15-16).

Practicing Discernment

We need to ask the Holy Spirit for discernment that is based on a foundational knowledge and understanding of God's Word:

For though by this time you ought to be teachers, you need someone to teach you again the first principles of the oracles of God; and you have come to need milk and not solid food. For everyone who partakes only of milk is unskilled in the word of righteousness, for he is a babe. But solid food belongs to those who are of full age, that is, those who by reason of use have their senses exercised to discern both good and evil (Hebrews 5:12-14).

If we receive a download from God through a dream or vision, we need to discern what the Holy Spirit is saying. Dreams and visions may be abstract, perhaps in the form of a riddle, and may be misunderstood or misinterpreted. For example, I was having a cup of coffee with a woman when she began to tell me that she was feeling a bit discouraged. She was on the prayer team at her church and was part of a meeting to pray about the church building. The lease was coming to an end and the owner was not going to renew it so they needed some direction.

As they prayed, this woman had a very strong vision in which she saw a building like theirs almost on top of a large train track. In the natural there actually was a train track about a mile from the existing church. In great excitement the woman spoke it out. Everyone jumped into their cars to drive down to the area she saw in the vision. They drove around looking for the building she had seen, but there were no commercial buildings only domestic properties. The woman was embarrassed. She thought she had missed the message and was now unsure about dreams and visions. I assured her that she hadn't missed the message of the vision, only misinterpreted it. I told her that the Lord was speaking to her in a riddle. He had used the natural circumstances and environment, such as the train tracks that were close by, to say that He was going to bring the lease "back on track." Sure enough, the landlord changed his mind and the lease was renewed.

As Christians we should be careful how we interpret the downloads we receive from God. We need to ask the Holy Spirit for wisdom and discernment to interpret what He is saying.

Summary

- The chain of command in the spirit realm means angels are waiting for us to call them forth by decreeing God's revelatory word.

- Humans are like radio receivers—sensitive to frequencies in the spirit realm.

- Our tongue carries power to bless or curse.

- We may ignorantly decree a curse by agreeing with the plans of the enemy.

- At times we pick up activity in the heavenlies such as depression and lust. These may be words of knowledge if you have dealt with these issues.

- Disturbing images may be God wanting to set people free.

- Animals are sensitive to the spirit realm.

- Ask the Holy Spirit for discernment based on a foundational knowledge and understanding of God's Word.

Endnote

1. See book titles listed in the front of this book.

CHAPTER 5

WHO QUALIFIES?

Adrian Beale

Who Qualifies to Work With Angels?

Who qualifies to interact with angels is best related through the historical accounts recorded in the Old Testament. When Hagar had conceived by Abram and fled from her mistress Sarai, she was visited by an angel in the wilderness. Even though she had not yet given birth to Abram's son, the angel told her to return to her mistress and God would multiply her seed (Genesis 16:7-11). The angel visited Hagar based solely on the promise God had made to Abram earlier, that He would multiply his seed as the stars of heaven (Genesis 15:4-5).

The angelic visitation Hagar received was not for her benefit but for the welfare of the seed she carried (Genesis 21:13). That it was all about the promise to Abraham's seed is later reiterated when Hagar and Ishmael (her son) were sent away after the birth of Isaac. At that time Hagar once again found herself in the wilderness and was visited by an angel. However, on this occasion, even though Hagar lifted up her voice in despair, it was not her voice that was heard by God, it was Ishmael's cries that reached God's ears:

> *And the water in the skin was used up, and she placed the boy under one of the shrubs. Then she went and sat down across from him at a distance of about a bowshot; for she said to herself, "Let me not see the death of the boy." So she sat opposite him, and lifted her voice and wept. And God heard the voice of the lad. Then the angel of God called to Hagar out of heaven, and said to her, "What ails you, Hagar? Fear not, for God has heard the voice of the lad where he is"* (Genesis 21:15-17).

This is an important distinction, it tells us that angelic intervention is primarily for the sons of Abraham. While this initially speaks of Abraham's physical lineage, as was witnessed earlier in the Six-Day

War, it also includes those who have faith in Christ. Paul, writing to the Galatian church, confirms our inclusion, when he says:

> *Understand, then, that those who have faith are chil-*
> *dren of Abraham. Scripture foresaw that God would*
> *justify the Gentiles by faith, and announced the gospel*
> *in advance to Abraham: "All nations will be blessed*
> *through you." So those who rely on faith are blessed*
> *along with Abraham, the man of faith* (Galatians 3:7-9;
> see also Romans 4:16-18).

Therefore, as sons of God and heirs of Abraham through faith in the finished work of the Cross we should believe for and expect angelic intervention. As new covenant believers we can be assured that we qualify, and angelic activity is just a normal part of everyday Kingdom living.

What Robs and Blinds Us to Angelic Activity

There are constant, covert spiritual battles taking place in the heavenlies every day, and God assigns seasoned intercessors an incredibly important role in working with and directing His army in this unseen war (Daniel 10:13,20-21; Matthew 22:44; Acts 12:12). However, even if we are not called into an intercessory role, it is also important to understand there are certain beliefs and dispositions that will blind us to angelic activity at a personal level.

Ignorance of His Current Reign

Angels are servants of the King of Glory, who is the King of a Kingdom in operation right now. While that may be obvious to some, to others who have been conditioned to expect only a future kingdom fulfillment, it places His heavenly servants beyond their current grid of understanding.[1] As a consequence, this latter group will likely have no expectation and personal experience with the current intervention of angels. In effectively deferring the power of God to a future dispensation, they have limited its display today. The Scriptures not only point out that angels do God's bidding,

> *Bless the Lord, you His angels, who excel in strength, who do His word, heeding the voice of His word* (Psalm 103:20).

They also necessarily precede this declaration with His enthronement:

> *The Lord has established His throne in heaven, and His kingdom rules over all* (Psalm 103:19).

For without recognition of His enthronement there will be little appreciation for His jurisdiction and the role played by angels working with His sons and daughters.

Cessationists

Sharing much of this debilitating mindset are Cessationists, those who believe the power of God is no longer available today, having apparently died with the apostles in the first century. Like the Sadducees before them, this group disempower God by centering their religious expression rigidly on repetitive doctrine void of revelation that displays the Father heart of God.

In the Gospels, Jesus ironically called out this sect as those not knowing the Scriptures or the power of God (Matthew 22:29). While today this group may qualify as sons of Abraham through an acknowledgment of the Cross, their unbelief, on the other hand, denies them access to Kingdom living and provision.

Lack of a Humble Hunger

Finally, having looked at the role of angels as bearers of revelation, revisiting an earlier verse will close out our discussion:

> So He **humbled** you, allowed you to **hunger**, and fed you with manna which you did not know nor did your fathers know, that He might make you know that man shall not live by bread alone; but man lives by every word that proceeds from the mouth of the Lord (Deuteronomy 8:3).

This verse not only serves to define manna as that which proceeds out of the mouth of the Lord, it also provides the two attitudes required to receive it. Thus, the two words in bold highlight the necessary inner ground upon which revelation is deposited. In doing so, it indirectly warns that their opposites will rob us of life-giving revelation, and, of course, interaction with the angels that are sent to deliver it. Humility according to a scriptural search is related to the heart or spirit of man, while hunger is an expression of the soul. Together they are the collective that makes up the inner man. Remember, God deliberately introduced manna as Israel traversed the wilderness:

> They wandered in the wilderness in a solitary way; they found no city to dwell in. Hungry and thirsty, their soul fainted in them. Then they cried unto the Lord in their trouble, and he delivered them out of their distresses. And he led them forth by the right way, that they might go to a city of habitation (Psalm 107:4-7 KJV).

Why was the wilderness the setting to present manna? God poetically introduced the importance of revelation in the wilderness because the word "wilderness" (midbar) has two remarkably diverse meanings: first it does refer to a desert, but it also describes the mouth as a human instrument of speech. What this conveys is that the mouth is the entry point to the kingdom and that without revelation what proceeds from the human mouth is but a wilderness!

When we speak divinely released insight (the rhema word of revelation), His words spoken through us create Kingdom provision. Recognizing the stark barrenness of the wilderness is meant to develop humility and hunger for God's best within us. While each may offer their own definition of humility, what is spoken of here is not something shown outwardly, but rather a personal spiritual dependency on God marked by prayer (2 Chronicles 7:14).

Hunger, on the other hand, as depicted in the Psalm 107 verse, could be described as a serious lack of food that earnestly pulls on God to meet the void of a famished soul. Therefore, people who are hungering after riches (like Balaam), those who are spiritually complacent, and know-all type personalities are likely blind to angelic activity (Numbers 22:18-34; 1 Corinthians 1:26).

Summary

- Angelic interaction is primarily for the sons of Abraham.

- We are children of Abraham by faith in Jesus Christ.

- What blinds us to angelic activity:
  - Ignorance of His current reign
  - Cessationist mindset
  - Lack of humble hunger

- Speaking divinely released insights creates Kingdom provision.

- The wilderness develops humility and hunger.

- Riches, complacency, and know-it-all personalities are likely blinded to angelic activity.

Endnote

1. The external nature of the Kingdom as a now and future Kingdom is fully discussed in the book *Kingdom Mysteries: Hidden in Plain Sight—Your Invitation to Access and Release Heaven's Provision* by Adrian Beale.

CHAPTER 6

ANGEL ENCOUNTERS

Adam F. Thompson

I have talked about the heavenlies and how we can sense demonic activities—but the heavenlies are also home to the angelic realm and therefore we may interact with angels, which are ministering spirits. In some streams of the Church this has led to accusations of the heresy of worshipping angels as referred to in Colossians:

> *Let no one keep defrauding you of your prize by delighting in self-abasement and the worship of angels, taking his stand on visions he has seen, inflated without cause by his fleshly mind, and not holding fast to the head, from whom the entire body...grows with a growth which is from God* (Colossians 2:18-19 NASB).

So before we discuss interaction with angels sent by God, we will address the foundations of the heresy of worshipping them.

In an earlier chapter, I likened angels to being employees of the Kingdom, which is like an eternal family business. It's not too great a stretch of the imagination to believe that there are even living quarters provided for the angels as loyal employees in the business! But angels will never be heirs to the business or have the authority exercised by heirs. The sons and daughters of God, as coheirs with Jesus Christ, receive free access to all of the "company perks" because one day they will inherit everything and run the family business.

Lucifer, not satisfied with being a high-level management employee, objected to this arrangement and was dismissed from the company along with other disgruntled workers. Ever since that time, lucifer, now referred to as satan, has been actively recruiting men and women to serve him, not God. This explains why some people, especially those involved in New Age practices, tend to worship angels.

Putting angels on pedestals is a profanity because they are only the workers or employees of Heaven. Only the children of God are His heirs. Jesus is the firstborn Son and is the heir to the throne of

God; but we, too, are the children of the living God, which makes us coheirs with Him.

I can't say it too many times: Jesus didn't come to earth to die for angels, He died for humankind, for the sons and daughters of the living God! He has redeemed us by His blood to be part of His family and His inheritance. Part and parcel of the beauty and power of the Cross is that we have been made heirs to the throne of God, giving us the authority to work with angels by decreeing His Word. Angels are commissioned by the Father to serve us because we are kings, priests, and prophets in the Kingdom of God. This blessing is our inheritance through the intimacy of knowing Him.

Interacting With Angels

When God opens the eyes of our understanding, He sends angels that we can see beyond the veil. We may literally see robed angels as beings, with or without wings, but we may also sense-see angels in visions, trances, and in dreams.

Interacting with angels is often a controversial subject. People sometimes tell me that we don't have the authority to tell angels what to do, but I have to correct them. It is our privilege as children of God to work with and marshal angels. This authority comes through knowing our inheritance in God. We are heirs to the throne by the revelation of Jesus Christ and by faith in what He has done. It is in His righteousness and by focusing on the truth that we are in Him and He is in us, that we have Kingdom authority. By faith we set our minds on the things that are above. If we are in that revelatory realm, we can assign angels to do His Word through prayer. As it says in Psalm 103:

> *Bless the Lord, you His angels, who excel in strength,*
> *who do His word, heeding the voice of His word. Bless*
> *the Lord, all you His hosts, you ministers of His, who do*

His pleasure. Bless the Lord, all His works, in all places of His dominion. Bless the Lord, O my soul! (Psalm 103:20-22)

According to other Bible translations, the angels *"perform"* His Word. If we operate out of that revelatory understanding and start to decree His Word, the angels will obey and interact with us. The armies of heaven will be released against the powers of the enemy to prepare the way; for the Bible says that angels will be sent ahead of us for those who inherit salvation. The revelation of our inheritance in Jesus Christ is that we can mobilize angels when our vocabulary lines up with God's Word, as previously mentioned.

Various Representations of Angels

There may be different manifestation of angels, either in open visions or in our dreams. In our books, *The Divinity Code* and *God's Prophetic Symbolism in Everyday Life,* Adrian Beale and I discuss how God speaks to us using metaphors and symbols. The use of symbols is the language of heaven and so the Lord may speak to us by sending an angel that is in the form of something or someone else. The angel may not appear with wings and wearing a white robe, but may appear as an image of somebody we respect and honor in the natural. In other words, God may use such a person to represent an angel in a dream.

Depending on the context of the dream, that angel-representation can even represent Jesus, the Son of God, particularly if His name is Chris. Taking the context of the dream into account, it could be interpreted that Jesus is speaking to you. Another example is seeing an angel in the form of a person you know to be a prophet. This is most likely a representation of the Holy Spirit.

It might seem strange to accept that some angels look like humans, but the biblical record is clear. For example, when Peter was released from prison and went to the house where the disciples were praying for his release, they didn't believe it was him. Scripture records that they thought it must be his angel:

> *And as Peter knocked at the door of the gate, a girl named Rhoda came to answer. When she recognized Peter's voice, because of her gladness she did not open the gate, but ran in and announced that Peter stood before the gate. But they said to her, "You are beside yourself!" Yet she kept insisting that it was so. So they said, "It is his angel"* (Acts 12:13-15).

It can be deduced from this passage that Peter's angel looked like him. I would suggest therefore that if an angel can cross over from the spirit realm into the natural realm and have a physical form in the natural sense, then I believe God can do it in our dreams, too. This is just an example of how God speaks in metaphors and riddles.

Dream Encounters of the Night

There is a different type of dream, which is a *dream encounter*. These occur when God speaks to us through a literal visitation of an angel. In an earlier chapter where I spoke of various angelic roles, I described how a revelatory angel gave me direction for transition into full-time ministry. I described being awakened from sleep to see my physical body still lying on my bed, and walking into another room where I saw hundreds of angels surrounding the house in a misty cloud of glory. Even though it was dark I could see all of this angelic activity around me, as if I was wearing night vision goggles. That was a dream encounter.

Another such dream encounter took place in early 2012. I was asleep when an angel literally manifested in a very dramatic manner. The windows burst open, the curtains billowed, and a rushing wind ushered the angel toward me. The angel was dressed in white and had dark, shoulder-length hair. He came toward me with a sword saying, "I come from the presence of God with the word from the living God. The Lord wants you to know that when you and Todd meet together and pray, whatever you ask for will be done and nothing will get in the way of that prayer." The message was very simple and I was familiar with the Bible verse:

> *Again I say to you that if two of you agree on earth concerning anything that they ask, it will be done for them by My Father in heaven* (Matthew 18:19).

It was a powerful and unforgettable encounter. When I described this angel to a prophet friend, he suggested that the angel might have been Gabriel, the announcing angel. He explained that, in his experience, Gabriel has always appeared with black, shoulder-length hair and always says that he comes from the presence of God.

Since then, everything Todd Weatherly and I have agreed on in prayer to God has been released to us. The following story is one example that testifies to this. We were praying for God to provide finances for a building fund because we were in the process of looking for property to purchase and we needed money for a deposit. God, out of His grace, released into the church bank account a deposit of $500,000 specifically for the building fund. We didn't set up fund-raising events. We didn't beg people for money or manipulate people into giving. We just met and agreed together according to the word of the Lord. Whatever we asked for the Lord provided, exactly as announced by the angelic encounter in my dream. Through His grace the Lord has continued to honor our requests.

Angels in Open Visions

Angels sometimes appear in open visions, where our eyes are wide open. I often experience this while I am ministering. I can actually pinpoint where the angels are standing. I can see them in the spirit, which is not like looking with the natural or naked eye, but is using our spiritual senses to have the eyes of our understanding wide open. When people are positioned under an open heaven of angels they will receive impartations, experience deliverance, and be healed.

During a time of ministry in Australia's capital city, Canberra, I was indicating particular individuals and naming their ailments and sicknesses through words of knowledge. Afterward, one young man came up to me to describe an open vision he experienced in the meeting; it was the first time this had happened to him. This young man saw an angel standing next to me pointing toward the people as I was calling them out. He was quite stunned because he knew he was seeing beyond the veil and into the heavenlies. This experience of seeing into the heavenlies is available to you, too. When the eyes of your understanding are opened, you have the ability to see angels.

In New Zealand, I was praying for a woman's back to be restored and healed. I decreed the presence of a healing angel because I believe the healing angels minister the revelation of healing power from the Lord Jesus Christ as described in Isaiah 53—by His stripes we are healed. Adrian Beale was standing next to me, holding the microphone. He literally felt this healing angel push him and the microphone aside so that it could get to the woman and usher in the healing power of the Lord Jesus Christ. Adrian was taken aback by how forcefully the healing power of God was released when the healing angel was decreed.

While ministering in a church in North Carolina, I sensed a revelatory angel—the one who releases visions—was standing behind me and sort of leaning on me as I called to the front a married couple who were unable to have children. They told me their barrenness was so absolute that they had already adopted children. But as the angel leaned in to me I saw, prophetically, a baby boy and the Lord showed me that the woman would give birth to this child. I remembered Hannah who gave birth to Samuel, the prophet, and Elizabeth who bore John the Baptist, the one who ushered in the coming Christ. I was reminded how often God has used barren women to convey a message to His people.

In the presence of the revelatory angel, what I see in the spirit is always more real than what I see literally with my natural eyes. As it says in Second Corinthians 4:18, we are not to rely on what we see with the natural eye, but we are to act according to the eternal realm that has more substance than the temporal. When we do that, we are actually pulling on Heaven, calling things out of the invisible and into the physical; calling those things that are not as though they are (Romans 4:17).

When I'm ministering, I stand in that realm where I have come through the gate under the cascade of the angelic—a realm where more is revealed and I see very clearly. It's like standing on a mountaintop and having a 360-degree view of the horizon in every direction. When you see more, you can decree with confidence because the eternal realm has eternal energy and no time zone. When you start to decree in the power of the Holy Spirit, eternal law overrides natural law, and the natural has to align with the eternal. This is when we see miracles.

I was back at that same church in North Carolina some two years later and discovered that the barren couple had become the parents of a son, just as the vision had shown me. There was no need for them to email me to tell me it had happened. When you act in the prophetic you just leave the outworking of it to God and He gets the glory.

I want to encourage you that as a believer, you may see angels in dreams, trances, or open visions; and when you do, you have the authority in Jesus Christ to decree the atmosphere in which miracles take place.

Summary

- We are not called to worship angels.

- We may see angels as beings with or without wings.

- We may also sense-see angels in dreams, visions, and trances.

- When we decree the revelatory word, angels go into action.

- Angels may appear in the form of something or someone else.

- God can use a person to represent an angel, particularly in dreams.

- Angels may look like regular people.

- Dream encounters are literal visitations and may involve angelic interaction.

- What we see by revelation is more real than what we see in the natural.

- The natural laws have to align with what you are seeing in the eternal realm.

- When angels appear in a dream, vision, or trance, you will receive an authority to decree what they are relaying from God.

CHAPTER 7

PORTALS

Adrian Beale

Geographic Portals

We had just sat down to eat at an alfresco restaurant on a Melbourne sidewalk, when a few minutes later Adam went into one of his blank-stare moments. I knew he was having a vision. When he came out of it, I asked him what he had seen. He said with a measure of concern, "A spirit of death." This wasn't the first time I had heard him say that, so we continued our meal and waited till our server came to our table to ask whether there had been any unusual spiritual activity at this location.

Sure enough, when he came to our table the waiter kindly obliged by explaining that the building next door used to be a brothel and that one of the girls became pregnant by the owner. His angry wife had set fire to the building wanting to destroy the mother and baby, and as a result people had died. On top of this, the waiter said, "Last year a woman fell down the stairs out back and was killed." He went on to say, "In fact, this place is part of Melbourne's ghost tour because of the activity here." Adam and I turned to each other with confirmatory looks and continued to eat our meal.

A couple of guys were seated to our right and two women were sharing a drink and a plate of tapas at a table on our left. Suddenly the men's conversation became overbearingly loud. It became clear that our presence had stirred something in the spirit realm because the subject of their ever-encroaching exchange was the speculative "Gospel of Thomas." Their mutual goading came to a crescendo with, "How can you trust the Bible because in Thomas' Gospel, God is portrayed as a woman?!" We looked at each other knowing this was too coincidental to be coincidental and began to pray in the Spirit before decreeing the spirits using these two glove puppets to be quiet! We did this firmly but without shouting or making a scene. Sure enough, a minute or so later their conversation quelled like the wind had been taken from their sails.

Almost on cue the women to our left began a conversation that similarly became obnoxiously loud. The subject of their railing was the church. They were feeding off each other as they derided specific churches and their leadership, by name. Adam and I dealt with that situation in the same way we had silenced the men moments earlier.

What had we just experienced? We were simply out having some downtime looking for a meal when we happened across a portal that was open for enemy activity. Nefarious activity at this location had obviously opened a door through which evil spirits could exert anti-Christ influence using suitable human vessels.

There are both godly and ungodly portals on planet Earth through which angels—evil and elect—seek to influence our world. Unlike their evil counterpart, angels seek to work in harmony with God through believers who understand their role in bringing heaven to earth. This chapter endeavors to aid our understanding of this divinely appointed relationship.

Moses' Tabernacle

After Jacob's experience at Bethel, the next major place where we encounter one of these interdimensional gateways is in the record of building Moses' tabernacle. Why was Moses under strict instructions to build the tabernacle in accordance with what he had seen on the mount (Hebrews 8:5)? Why was such emphasis and detail laid upon its construction? I am not denying the powerful parallel between our body, soul, and spirit and the three courts of the tabernacle. However, beyond that revelation, it was imperative that it be duplicated to the letter because a portal existed between these parallel worlds of heaven and earth.

When Aaron stepped into the Most Holy Place, he stepped through an eternal veil and found himself in the very presence of God. Conversely, the reverse was also true, God, who is Spirit, dwelt among humans by inhabiting the tabernacle and temple. There was a connection or eternal pathway between the earthly housing and its spiritual counterpart.

Just as Adam and I encountered spiritual activity in a certain downtown Melbourne location, it is not uncommon because of an association or use of certain buildings and locations to experience the same wherever you happen to be. You may sense liberty and the presence of God in places of worship and prayer because a door into heaven has been established. Thus, when Adam and I were permitted to go upstairs in Aimee Semple McPherson's cabin at Lake Tahoe, California, we could tangibly feel God's presence in the place. Alternatively, you may feel uncomfortable, sense evil, or have ungodly dreams in a place, like a motel, where they rent rooms by the hour. Just as Jacob encountered angels ascending and descending at Bethel (Genesis 28:12), understand that there are geographic locations where spiritual portals exist and will influence those who frequent them.

Godly Portals Can Change Hands

It is also important to point out that the enemy seeks to close and encamp on portals that were at one time godly in nature. The Holy of Holies in Solomon's temple, which once was a place where the high priest would enter the very presence of God, has today become a place of dispute and contention through which anti-Christ forces seek to exert their influence.

Similarly, Los Angeles, the City of Angels, must once have borne the hopes of those who named it. However, LA today, recognized as the entertainment capital of the world, is for the most part a stronghold for the enemy seeking to multiply its influence through ungodly movie production. That is not to say there aren't godly elements seeking to redeem it, but simply take a walk down Hollywood

Boulevard and you quickly see and feel the type of spirits seeking expression in this place.

A word of warning, don't go looking to confront and close an ungodly portal unless you receive revelation and are called to do so. I know someone who tried to strut their stuff and close a witches' coven, without being called to do so, only to find themselves in the hospital with a life-threatening ailment a week later.

People as Portals

At one time Jesus made a detour across the Sea of Galilee with His disciples specifically to deal with a principality that exerted controlling influence well beyond the region of the Gadarenes (Mark 4:35–5:20). The buffeting their boat experienced as they made their way is testament to the extent of influence held by the demonic forces they were yet to encounter face to face. In choosing to side-step from His successful ministry (Matthew 8:16-18), Jesus' immediate return after legion's deliverance (Mark 5:21), and in particular, His questioning of the disciples' faith mid-journey (Matthew 8:26; John 5:19), all combine to confirm Jesus had received a specific word to shut down this territorial spirit. Not only was legion territorial, as an individual he was also acting as a portal through which the demonic sought to exert influence.

Mediums act as conduits in the same way for the demonic today. While legion could not be restrained by natural means (Mark 5:4), he was readily overcome by someone drawing from a superior spiritual armory, namely the living word of God. The contrast of earthly chains against Jesus' word that set this strongman free demonstrates that real binding and loosing is spiritual in nature and is achieved through the delivery of God-inspired and infused words of revelation.

Human Temples

In reference to portals, Jesus quoted from Jacob's experience at Bethel when He spoke to Nathaniel in John's Gospel, *"Truly, truly, I say to you, you will see heavens opened and the angels of God ascending and descending on the Son of Man"* (John 1:51 NASB).

While Jesus was likely alluding to His ministry that was to follow and the door opened through His death upon the Cross, on another level in speaking in this way, He was also bridging religious minds to the idea that the temple (Bethel: the house of God) made of stone was but a prelude to God's plan of replacing it with human temples. Even though, at the time, His hearers missed it, He was certainly more direct on this point when He said, *"Destroy this temple, and in three days I will raise it up"* (John 2:19 NASB).

Ultimately, through Jesus' sacrifice, believers were cleansed so that they themselves could become human temples of the Holy Spirit and thus portals of God. Therefore, in saying, *"For indeed, the kingdom of God is within you"* (Luke 17:21), Jesus was declaring that believers are themselves walking gateways to another realm. When you and I enter into an arena to minister, we are not alone—the fullness of the resources of heaven are at our disposal.

Portals of Heaven

Most Christians have heard leaders pray and dispatch angels to bring in the lost in accordance with a verse from the book of Hebrews, where it says, in reference to angels, *"Are they not all ministering spirits sent forth to minister for those who will inherit salvation?"* (Hebrews 1:14).

And while this is a legitimate rendering of the verse, it should be noted that the word, *"for"* is the Greek word *dia*, which means through. So the verse literally reads: *"Are they not all ministering spirits sent forth to minister through those who will inherit salvation."*

That one word change can make a world of difference, wouldn't you say? It is from this rendition that we can be deliberately provocative by saying, "Angels come to earth through your mouth!" While you may be trying to picture such a thing, let me explain that angels are dispatched by words expressed through our lips. These are not just any words. They are not even godly words with a religious origin. They are, however, words spoken by God Himself through us. Here the Bible says, *"Bless the Lord, you His angels, who excel in strength, who do His word, heeding the voice of His word"* (Psalm 103:20).

When God releases a rhema word of revelation (manna), whether it comes through reading the Scriptures, from a dream, vision, prophetic incident, or from a multitude of different avenues, the moment we line up our mouth with it, angels go to work. In this way we become conduits or portals of Heaven. As believers we are in two places at the same time. While our physical bodies may be here on earth, our spirit is seated in heavenly places.

Our heavenly self is as a star reflecting the glory of God to a darkened world. In that place God releases a word to us; and our role, as His children, is to decipher what He is saying to our spirit and relay it here on earth. In the process, angels are engaged to work in harmony with the word that is released, to see the promises of the Kingdom of Heaven become manifest on earth. In this way we work with the host of Heaven. This also means that when we enter an arena having first heard from Heaven, we automatically outrank the enemy.

The Messenger Carries the Same Authority as the One Who Sent Him

There are a multiple of places in Scripture where angels speak on behalf of God.[1] When they do so, they are not working to their own personal agenda, they are simply relaying God's word. As such, when they come with a word it is as God Himself speaking. Another way of looking at this is—the messenger carries the same authority as the One who sent him or her. Therefore when we hear from God and speak into a situation, it is not us speaking, but God speaking through us—and as a consequence angels go to work. Be mindful that when we are bearers of God's rhema word, very often we may face an initial resistance from the enemy; it is at those times we need to understand in whose authority we stand.

Summary

- There are geographic portals through which angels—evil and elect—seek to influence our world.

- The tabernacle was a portal between heaven and earth.

- Stepping into the Holy of Holies placed Aaron before the presence of God.

- Godly portals exist in places of worship.

- Ungodly portals exist in places of nefarious activity.

- Previous godly portals can change into the hands of the enemy.

- Do not attempt to shut down an ungodly portal unless you are called to do so by God.

- People may also act as portals.

- Binding and loosing is spiritual in nature and is achieved through the delivery of God's revelatory word.

- Believers cleansed through the blood of Christ are now temples and thus portals to another realm.

- As a portal, Heaven's resources go with you.

- Angels come to earth through your mouth—angels are dispatched by revelatory words that pass through your lips.

- As believers we are in two places at the same time. While our earthly body is here, our heavenly self is seated in heavenly places revealing God's glory to a darkened world.

- The messenger carries the same authority as the one who sent him or her.

Endnote

1. See Judges 2:1; 6:12; 13:16; 2 Samuel 24:16-17; 2 Kings 1:3-4; Zechariah 1:14; Luke 1:19,30,38; Revelation 22:6.

CHAPTER 8

STEPPING INTO KINGDOM POWER

Adam F. Thompson

I was not surprised to read a recent report about a newly formed church called Way of the Future. Apparently its sole purpose is to control the human race through Artificial Intelligence (AI) and is committed to creating a "peaceful and respectful transition of who is in charge of the planet from people to people and machines."[1] There is nothing new about the spirit of anti-Christ's intention to replace God and desensitize people to His miraculous power, for it has always tried to counterfeit heavenly authority and glorify humans.

God is not fazed by such attempts to counterfeit His power. On the contrary, God is raising up a company of believers who will move in an unprecedented realm of the supernatural. He is calling out a company of saints who will pursue the promise, as Abraham did, and move in the spirit and the power of Elijah. I can tell you now that this is not about emotional begging or an exhausting false bravado in prayer. It's about tapping into our God-given inheritance. It's about coming into revelation of our identity and stepping into the Kingdom.

Nathaniel

John the Baptist announced the Kingdom of Heaven with the words, *"Repent, for the kingdom is at hand!"* (Matthew 3:2). In other words, the Kingdom is as close as our fingertips. It was as close as that to Nathanael when Phillip brought him to meet the Lord. Philip told Nathanael, *"We have found Him of whom Moses in the law, and the prophets, wrote—Jesus of Nazareth, the son of Joseph"* (John 1:45).

And Nathanael said:

> *"Can any good thing come out of Nazareth?" Philip said*
> *to him, "Come and see." Jesus saw Nathanael coming to*
> *Him, and said of him, "Behold, an Israelite indeed, in*
> *whom there is no deceit!" Nathanael said to Him, "How*
> *do You know me?" Jesus answered and said to him,*

> *"Before Philip called you, when you were under the fig tree, I saw you." Nathanael answered Him, "Rabbi, You are the Son of God; You are the King of Israel." Jesus answered and said to him, "Because I said to you that I saw you under the fig tree, do you believe? You will see greater things than these." And He said to him, "Truly, truly, I say to you, you will see the heavens opened and the angels of God ascending and descending on the Son of Man"* (John 1:46-51 NASB).

I imagine Jesus smiling when He said of Nathanael, *"Here is a real Israelite; there is nothing false in him!"* (Good News Translation). And when Nathanael asked Jesus, *"How do You know me?"* and Jesus replied, *"when you were under the fig tree, I saw you,"* we understand that Jesus had seen Nathanael in the spirit.

I suggest that the fig tree was where Nathanael had his devotional times with God; the space where he found a place of communion in his spirit with the Spirit. It was where he encountered the Lord. I believe it wasn't so much the accuracy of the word of knowledge that moved Nathanael, but it was that he recognized he had encountered Jesus during his devotional times. It was an "It's You!" moment that caused him to confess faith in Jesus as the *"King of Israel."*

Jesus then prophesied that Nathanael would see angels ascending and descending to give glory to the Son of Man. In effect, Jesus was prophesying that Nathanael would be among those who would embrace the new order in Christ to be gates within the Gate.

> *To them God willed to make known what are the riches of the glory of this mystery among the Gentiles: which is Christ in you, the hope of glory* (Colossians 1:27).

As Adrian mentioned earlier, Jesus didn't say descending and ascending, but that ascending came first and then descending. There is a connection here to the use of sanctified imagination. When we decree the word of the Lord using our imaginations, we start to see the promises of God as a picture. Jesus Himself said He does only what He sees His Father doing (John 5:19). When we start to see the revelation of the Kingdom, we begin to decree it. And when we decree the word of the Lord in this way, angels will gather; because according to Psalm 103:20, their primary function is to do the bidding of the Word.

As we decree the word of the Lord, angels are released. They ascend into the heavenlies to pull the promises of the Kingdom out of the invisible realms and then they descend, interacting with the Holy Spirit to bring them into our physical environment.

Nathanael isn't prominent in the Gospels, so it would be easy to treat this story as a sideline; however, it tells us something important. Metaphorically, the fig tree under which Nathanael was sitting represented Israel. Jesus saw that Nathanael was a man tied to the old ways and so He used metaphoric language to explain that a change was coming that would make it possible to experience an open door between heaven and earth. This open door would allow us to draw from the Tree of Life just as was done in Eden; this is what living as a mature believer should look like.

In John 10:7-9, Jesus describes Himself as the door, or the gate as some versions of the Bible put it. As temples of the Holy Spirit, we align ourselves with the Eternal Door so that we become a gate within the Gate. Jesus is the Gate within believers who are called to be gates between heaven and earth.

Ambassadors

This revelation of who we are as ambassadors for the Kingdom of God is going to be a shock to many in the church. It is something many followers of Christ do not yet understand or practice. Those believers are saved by faith in their hearts and the confession of their lips, and the grace of God is on their lives—but they aren't aware of how to walk in the spirit. Walking in the spirit results from the intimacy found in being trees that are watered by the running stream of the word of the Lord. This is why the psalmist writes:

> *Blessed [fortunate, prosperous, and favored by God] is the man who does not walk in the counsel of the wicked [following their advice and example], nor stand in the path of sinners, nor sit [down to rest] in the seat of scoffers (ridiculers). But his delight is in the law of the Lord, and on His law [His precepts and teachings] he [habitually] meditates day and night. And he will be like a tree firmly planted [and fed] by streams of water, which yields its fruit in its season; its leaf does not wither; and in whatever he does, he prospers [and comes to maturity]* (Psalm 1:1-3 Amplified Bible).

We gain further insight into how we can walk in the spirit through the account of Jesus meeting the woman at the well (John 4:7-26). Old Testament law required the Jews to worship God in the temple, located in Jerusalem. The Samaritans had long ago settled for worshipping on the mountain because of the influence of their ungodly kings, but now Jesus was explaining to this Samaritan woman that the time was coming when people would worship God in the very courts of Heaven itself. In effect, He was saying that access to the presence of God would no longer be through religious rituals or designated places of worship. People would be able to pass through gates of thanksgiving and enter His very courts with praise, as described in Psalm 100. In our spirits, it would now be possible to recognize and activate the eternal love of God and come into one-on-one intimacy with the Father wherever we are located.

> *Jesus said to her, "Woman, believe Me, the hour is*
> *coming when you will neither on this mountain, nor in*
> *Jerusalem, worship the Father. You worship what you*
> *do not know; we know what we worship, for salvation*
> *is of the Jews. But the hour is coming, and now is, when*
> *the true worshipers will worship the Father in spirit and*
> *truth; for the Father is seeking such to worship Him.*
> *God is Spirit, and those who worship Him must worship*
> *in spirit and truth"* (John 4:21-24).

If we are content to be confined to earth's lower frequency, or atmosphere, our love will be superficial and will struggle to measure up to the eternal God who was, and is, and is to come. However, when we enter into eternity's atmosphere, or frequency, we can govern the Kingdom on earth even as it is in Heaven. We become doors, gates, and portals...with legs! This is one of the reasons Jesus taught His disciples to pray, *"Your kingdom come. Your will be done on earth as it is in heaven"* (Matthew 6:10).

Changing the Spiritual Atmosphere

One time when I was in Hong Kong, I had an experience of Heaven. As the apostle Paul said, I don't know if I experienced this in or out of my body, but during this heavenly encounter everything was worshipping. It came in glorious sound waves of love. Even when I came out of the encounter, those sound waves stayed with me. You see, when we become portals with legs, bringing heaven to earth, we change the spiritual atmosphere of the locality where we live. When we walk into a meeting or into a city, the atmosphere will change; and when the atmosphere is changed, everything in heaven joins with everything in time, space, and matter to give glory to God.

The atmosphere of Jerusalem changed just before Passover, when Jesus rode into the city on a donkey. Luke records:

> *And as He went, many spread their clothes on the road. Then, as He was now drawing near the descent of the Mount of Olives, the whole multitude of the disciples began to rejoice and praise God with a loud voice for all the mighty works they had seen, saying: "Blessed is the King who comes in the name of the Lord! Peace in heaven and glory in the highest!"* (Luke 19:36-38)

The people laid palm fronds at His feet and burst into loud cries, *Hosanna in the highest, blessed is He who comes in the name of the Lord.* They were giving high praise to God. Even little children entered into this extravagant worship. The Pharisees, men of the flesh, were offended because Jesus had brought about a dramatic change in the spiritual atmosphere and opened the way for the entire city to walk through into realms of glory. Because they could not control what happened, they feared their authority would be undermined. They had put God in a box of their own making and His manifest presence challenged everything they thought they were entitled to.

Some of the Pharisees in the crowd called out to Him to rebuke His disciples. The Pharisees were shocked by what the disciples were saying.

And some of the Pharisees called to Him from the crowd, *"Teacher, rebuke Your disciples."* Jesus answered them with a quote taken from Habakkuk 2:11: *"I tell you that if these should keep silent, the stones would immediately cry out."* Jesus knew that everything—everything!—felt the compulsion to worship because His very presence affected the atmosphere in the city. He was the Gate, the Door to heavenly realms so that earth could join with heaven in giving glory to God.

I am convinced the time is coming when corporate groups of believers will demonstrate Jesus' absolute authority before world leaders. Scripture describes Daniel in this way. The life of Daniel has particular lessons for us in the final countdown to the return of Jesus to planet Earth. We read that Daniel and his friends had great influence with Nebuchadnezzar, a king who was known as the most demonically ruthless ruler of his era. No other kingdom on earth was more powerful, yet the supernatural authority wielded by Daniel showed this earthly king that the Kingdom of the Eternal God is much greater.

Nebuchadnezzar went mad when he discovered just how puny his power was compared with God's. He spent seven years in a wilderness of utter powerlessness, even though God allowed his throne and kingdom to be maintained. Eventually Nebuchadnezzar was converted, restored to his right mind, and gave public honor to God.

Similar events will take place in the lead up to Christ's Second Coming. We will see believers empowered to appear before world leaders, just as Daniel was. Such empowerment will be imperative in a world where the increase in technology will counterfeit and attempt to replace the power of God. Simulation technology will deceive people into believing they are living in reality. People will be so desensitized to God's supernatural power that they will no longer be able to discern truth from fantasy.

Summary

- God is calling forth a company of saints in the spirit and power of Elijah.

- Nathaniel under the fig tree before meeting Jesus metaphorically paints a picture of someone coming out from under the old system unto Jesus, the Tree of Life.

- Jesus is the Door; as such, we are gates within a Gate.

- Jesus announced to the woman at the well that believers will no longer be confined to religious rituals and designated places of worship. Through Christ's death, we are able to pass through the gates of thanksgiving and enter His very courts with praise.

- Jesus' presence changes the spiritual atmosphere.

- Like Daniel, God is raising believers to speak and demonstrate authority on the world stage.

Endnote

1. Summer Meza, "Religion That Worships Artificial Intelligence Wants Machines to be in Charge of the Planet," *Newsweek*, November 17, 2017; https://www.newsweek.com/google -executive-forms-religion-artificial-intelligence-714416; accessed April 22, 2020.

CHAPTER 9

TONGUES OF ANGELS

Adrian Beale

Though I speak with the tongues of men and of angels, *but have not love, I am become as sounding brass or a clanging cymbal.*

1 CORINTHIANS 13:1

Mental Roadblocks

Very often the thing that stops people from breaking through into receiving the Baptism of the Spirit with the evidence of speaking in tongues is a mental block placed there by the influence of a religious spirit. With that understanding, in wanting to explain the link between tongues and angels, it is important for us to lay out and establish something of its scriptural foundation.

From the outset, be aware, that like the Sadducees who denied the resurrection and the work of angels (Acts 23:8), if you were to ask those who decry speaking in tongues about when Christ's Kingdom will come into effect they will likely project the Kingdom into some past or future dispensation. In doing so they inadvertently reveal that they are unaware of the eternal and current nature of the Kingdom of Heaven and therefore will also be blind to the current work of angels. After all, if you don't believe the King is on the throne now, then you are also unlikely to perceive and receive the working of His servants, the angels (Psalm 103:19-20).[1]

The opening chapter verse, First Corinthians 13:1, says that believers speak with the tongues of men and angels. Could Paul, who wrote this verse, be using the term *angels* beyond a mere contrasting range of purity—from mortals to the gilded tongues of angels? How could we know? What does context suggest? Paul deliberately sandwiched a chapter on love, of which this is its opening verse, between chapters 12 and 14 in the book of First Corinthians, both of which provide instruction in moving in the gifts of the Spirit. He did this to emphasize the heart from which the gifts are to operate.

After laying this accent on love, Paul continues in chapter 14 to highlight the operation and importance of speaking in tongues by dedicating over half the chapter to this expression of the Spirit. Therefore, it could be argued he wasn't just speaking in a figurative sense but was actually speaking literally. Thus at times when I am speaking in tongues, it may really be that I am speaking in an angelic language. You have to wonder for what purpose?

The Bridge to Eternal Truth

To take this further, we need to appreciate that if our understanding of the Kingdom of God is based solely on New Testament teaching, then we do not yet grasp the significance of its *eternal* nature. To access the fullness of eternity, we need to cross this divide and recognize that both Old and New Testaments provide an equal and complementary supply. Think about it, Jesus taught for forty days about the Kingdom after His resurrection (Acts 1:3), this was before the New Testament had been penned. Upon what did He base His teaching?

Jericho

In an earlier chapter we made a brief mention of the unseen nature of the work of angels by referencing Joshua's victory at Jericho. At that time Joshua met with the Lord of hosts, a term referring to the Commander of the armies of heaven. In his meeting, he was given a very specific and counterintuitive set of instructions on how the battle to take Jericho was to be fought. Though angels are not openly seen at Jericho's fall, Joshua's prior audience with the Lord of hosts and the supernatural way the walls fell—without human hands— almost certainly reveals that angels were involved in its demise.

The Use of Trumpets

Cutting to the chase, it should be noted that trumpets played a prominent role in the instruction given by Joshua.[2] If you recall, there were seven priests bearing seven shofars (trumpets) preceding the ark of the covenant as the men of war encircled the city thirteen times over the period of seven days (Joshua 6:4-15). It can be reasoned that the sound coming from the trumpets in the mouths of Joshua's priests is the Old Testament equivalent of speaking in tongues. How? Well, the book of Revelation tells us that the sound of a trumpet is a *"voice"* (Revelation 4:1).

And while it could be argued from this reference the voice like a trumpet may primarily be speaking about its volume, there is a strong parallel presented in Scripture between the Spirit of God and trumpets elsewhere. Thus we find in reference to Gideon, *"... the Spirit of the Lord came upon Gideon, and he blew a trumpet..."* (Judges 6:34).

This is further reinforced when Gideon's 300 men face the Midianites with trumpets in their mouths and torches in hands. So that when he and his men declare, *"The sword of the Lord and of Gideon!"* (Judges 7:20), we are drawn to conclude the trumpets on their lips symbolized the sword of the Spirit (Ephesians 6:17).

It is not without reason, then, that later in Israel's history when a remnant was rebuilding the walls of Jerusalem, Nehemiah described the scene by saying, *"Every one of the builders had his sword girded at his side as he built. And the one who sounded the trumpet was beside me"* (Nehemiah 4:18).

While in the natural that could be a throw-away line, given this discussion, when we reassess it through spiritual eyes and acknowledge the One who sounded the trumpet speaks of the Holy Spirit, we are equipped with a totally new appreciation for Nehemiah's later declaration, *"Wherever you hear the sound of the trumpet. ...Our God will fight for us"* (Nehemiah 4:20).

So it was not merely coincidental that when choosing a metaphor to describe speaking in tongues without an interpretation, and there were surely a plethora of options, the apostle Paul again deliberately chose a trumpet as his go-to image, *"For if the trumpet makes an uncertain sound, who will prepare for battle?"* (1 Corinthians 14:8).

Overcoming a Dispensational Mindset

Our difficulty in seeing such parallels between Old and New Testaments is hampered by a dispensational mindset. A "that was under the law and now we are under grace" type thinking. We default to that mindset because we fail to understand that eternity is not outside time, it is the fullness of time. We are no longer under the law. However, while chronologically the Old Testament is a historical account, in the light of the Cross, it is also an eternal account.

This is really important, so please let me explain by way of example. The year of Jubilee was God's divine reset button and figuratively the Year of Redemption. This year was accompanied by a proclamation of liberty throughout the land, when each person returned to their family and possessions, where debts were cancelled and slaves were set free (Leviticus 25). The Year of Jubilee commences with the Day of Atonement. Why? To answer that question it will help to ask another, "What is the greatest atonement?" Well, the Cross is the ultimate and greatest atonement in history, right?

Recognizing this fact, if we then insert the Cross into the day that marks the beginning of Jubilee and piece together that God was communicating an eternal truth, we can further see that the freedom and rest that followed this day was but a precursor to our day, where we also have had our debts cancelled, we have been set free from the bondage of sin, and we have been released to return to our eternal family and inheritance. Therefore, it is definitely more than by random chance that the Day of Atonement was marked by the blowing of trumpets (Leviticus 25:9) and that the New Testament records that *"where the Spirit of the Lord is, there is liberty"* (2 Corinthians 3:17). You see, the two are inextricably linked.

Two Types of Trumpet

Adding to this picture, in biblical Israel there were two type of trumpets—the shofar and the silver trumpet—that were used as signaling instruments for religious and secular ceremonies. And by the way, confirming an earlier statement, I believe the Bible actually teaches that both types are a voice, With (silver) trumpets and the voice of the shofar make a joyful noise before the Lord (see Psalm 98:6).

The silver trumpets were used as a signal when going to war and when making offerings and to mark new beginnings. Their use accompanied these occasions as a memorial, witness, and testimony before the Lord:

> *When you go to war in your land against the enemy who oppresses you, then you shall sound an alarm with the trumpets, and you will be remembered before the Lord your God, and you will be saved from your enemies. Also in the day of your gladness, in your appointed feasts, and at the beginning of your months, you shall blow the trumpets over your burnt offerings and over the sacrifices of your peace offerings; and they shall be a memorial for you before your God: I am the Lord your God* (Numbers 10:9-10).

Remember It's an Eternal Kingdom

The use of trumpets on these occasions caused God to remember Israel. The words, *"remembered"* and its cousin *"memorial"* used here are the Hebrew words *zakar* and *zikkaron*. respectively. *Zakar* has three main lines of thought: 1) To establish a memorial or sign; 2) to call to mind; and 3) to recite and invoke what has been called to mind. This is why Jesus called us to have communion in *remembrance* of Him (Luke 22:19).

To bring this into an eternal framework, it is important to acknowledge that Jesus is *"the Lamb slain from the foundation of the world"* (Revelation 13:8), and silver is the metal associated with redemption in Scripture (Leviticus 27:15,19; Numbers 3:48-51; 18:16; Isaiah 52:3). This means, though they doubtless did not understand it, when Israel blew their trumpets they were partaking of a victory not yet chronologically realized. They were entering into the triumph of the Cross before its time. Just as we partake of the provision of the Cross after the event, they were drawing from it before it had physically taken place.

This is the eternal Kingdom in operation. Now, outside of any learned signals, just as the actual voice emanating from a trumpet is beyond human comprehension, in a parallel way the language spoken by the Spirit in tongues is for the most part unrecognizable. Therefore, by apprehending the link between the Spirit, trumpets, and the representation of silver in Scripture, we can see spiritually that the use of silver trumpets is a picture of the Holy Spirit being given a voice through the redeemed.

In quick review:

- A trumpet has a voice.
- The Spirit is associated with the use of trumpets.
- Like the presence of the Spirit, the trumpet marks liberty.
- There is a parallel between the voice of the trumpet and the Holy Spirit.
- Silver trumpets signaled God to remember Israel during warfare and offerings.
- Silver is associated with redemption.
- To remember *(zakar)* means to: 1) establish a memorial; 2) call to mind; 3) declare and invoke.

- From an eternal perspective, Israel was partaking of Kingdom provision, only on the other side of the Cross.

- Putting this together, the use of silver trumpets prefigured the voice of the Holy Spirit through the redeemed declaring and invoking the victory of the Cross.

The Shofar

That said, when it comes to Jericho and Gideon's men defeating the Midianites, they were using shofars, not silver trumpets. When Gideon's 300 men blew their shofars, the Bible records, *"When the three hundred blew the trumpets* [shofars], *the Lord set every man's sword against his companion throughout the whole camp; and the army fled..."* (Judges 7:22).

This is not unlike the account where the Lord set ambushments against the enemy and they began destroying each other when Jehoshaphat sent forth singers to go ahead of the army (2 Chronicles 20:21-23). It appears that all three situations—Jehoshaphat, Gideon, and Joshua—invoked the assistance of angels. While it is not the focus of this study, when we understand that every Old Testament victory previews the Cross, we begin to apprehend from these scenes the panic and fear Christ's victory wrought in the enemies' camps. In the case of Gideon and Jehoshaphat's battles, unseen elements evidently brought division, confusion, and self-preservation to fever pitch among the enemy ranks. While for Joshua, the Lord's armies brought judgment upon the stronghold of sin in pulling down the walls of Jericho.

If these observations are correct, we need to ask, "What sets the shofar apart from the silver trumpet that it would direct angelic armies?" Perhaps it is the fact that the shofar is not man-made, but rather fashioned by the hand of God? What we do know about the shofar is that the Hebrew word for shofar is *sopar,* a ram's horn. The name appears to have been adopted from the Akkadian version of the Sumerian word for wild goat. The shofar is sounded every Friday night to begin the Sabbath; it is blown to announce the seventh month (Tishri), which is marked by the Feast of Trumpets; and its blasts declare the Year of Jubilee. What I find interesting is that each of these occasions signify the entry of rest. This suggests that wholesale angelic intervention, when it relates to speaking in tongues, takes place when what is released through our lips is revelatory.

The shofar parallels the words and songs in tongues that are no longer us priming the pump but direct input from on high. You know, that moment when it is no longer you speaking or singing and another has stepped into the room and is using you as His instrument. In these moments angels are being commissioned and directed to complete their assignments beyond any human bias and agenda.

In a day and age when there is religious reluctance to speaking in tongues, this chapter has been presented as a reasoned response opening something of its hidden scriptural foundation to encourage and embolden its use. Particularly in the field of corporate spiritual warfare it is time to harness our imagination using these Old Testament examples and exercise the gift, so that God may step into the room and display His supernatural glory. The angels are waiting.

Summary

- People who decry tongues, will likely also deny the work of angels.

- Those not understanding the eternal nature of the Kingdom will also miss the work of angels.

- When you speak in tongues, sometimes you are speaking the language of angels.

- Though unseen, Joshua's meeting with the Commander of the Lord's host strongly suggests angels were involved in Jericho's fall.

- Trumpets in the Old Testament are a parallel of speaking in tongues in the New.

- A "that was under the law and now we are under grace" mindset robs us of eternal Kingdom provision.

- There are many eternal parallels between the Old and New Testaments; Jubilee is an example.

- In blowing trumpets, Israel was partaking in the victory of the Cross before it had chronologically taken place.

- The moment it is not you speaking and another steps into the room and is using you as His instrument, angels are being dispatched to complete their assignment.

- Angels are waiting for us to exercise the spiritual gift of speaking in tongues.

Endnotes

1. The eternal nature of the Kingdom is more fully discussed in *Kingdom Mysteries, Hidden in Plain Sight* by Adrian Beale.

2. A full discussion of the battle of Jericho is found in Chapter 12 of *The Mystic Awakening* by Adrian Beale.

CHAPTER 10

STEPPING BEYOND THE NATURAL REALM

Adam F. Thompson

Activating Angels Through a Cascade of Worship

Worshipping the Lord is the gate into His presence. Jesus assures us that only through Him do we have legal access to the heavenly realms:

> *Jesus said to them again, "Truly, truly I say to you, I am the door of the sheep. All who came before Me are thieves and robbers, but the sheep did not hear them. I am the door; if anyone enters through Me, he will be saved, and go in and out and find pasture"* (John 10:7-9 NASB).

As recorded in Hebrews 1:14, angels are to serve God's people. Angels are activated to serve us when we worship God. However, there are also doors or gates into other spiritual realms. These gates may be opened through such things as trauma, fear, horror, or abuse. Even anxiety can open up the wrong gate. Let us make sure we open the right gates.

Genesis 27 records how Jacob's practice of deception opened the wrong gates and brought him under demonic influence. Jacob knew that Isaac's blessing was Esau's birthright, due to the fact that he was the firstborn of the twin boys—yet he chose to trick his brother into exchanging the birthright for a plate of stew. And then he went further, deceiving their father Isaac into conferring the blessing on himself, not Esau. Jacob's string of deception resulted in a harvest of deception in his life. His uncle Laban tricked him into marrying Leah instead of his first choice, Rachel, and then systematically cheated him by not paying him wages as promised. In activating the gate of deception, Jacob invited a curse on his life.

Jacob was passionate about having the blessing that was upon Abraham and Isaac. God honors passion for the spiritual seed that was in Abraham, but Jacob initially relied on deception, not faith in God, to get it. But I believe God saw Jacob's true heart for the blessing when Jacob wrestled with Him about it. In Genesis 28 we read how Jacob slept with his head on a rock and went into a dream encounter in which he met Jesus, who is the true Gate into the blessing. He saw the angels of God ascending and descending through that gate.

In John 4 Jesus spoke to the Samaritan woman by the well. He explained that the gate to God would no longer be found in geographically located temples, but only in the true Gate, the Portal of entrance, who is Jesus Christ. He went on to explain that we would worship in Spirit through the Gate, Jesus, who lives within us:

> *The hour is coming, and now is, when the true worshipers will worship the Father in spirit and truth; for the Father is seeking such to worship Him* (John 4:23).

When Jacob wrestled with God and saw the angels ascending and descending, he was seeing by faith the blessing of the land that God had promised Abraham and reiterated through Isaac. When Jacob became Israel, he was effectively seeing the Messiah as the Promised Land who would live within us in the New Covenant relationship. When Jacob rested his head on the rock, it was an act of surrender and intimacy that parallels John resting his head against the Rock, Jesus, in an act of worship on the eve of the crucifixion (John 13). This intimacy with his Lord led to the experience described in Revelation 4 where he saw a door opened in heaven through which he passed to stand in the very throne room of the Lord God Almighty.

This same John, who so understood intimate communion, recorded the story of Jesus telling Nathaniel how He saw him in intimate worship under the fig tree. What affected Nathaniel so strongly was not the word of knowledge as such, but the realization that this Jesus was the God of the universe that he encountered in his devotional times under the fig tree. And Jesus goes on to reference Jacob's experience of the angels ascending and descending. He tells

Nathaniel he will see greater things than those he saw in his devotions under the fig tree.

In other words, Jesus was telling Nathaniel what the New Covenant era would look like: Christ having been emptied on the Cross, having been cursed, would be the exchange for us to be filled and blessed with the *"fullness of the Godhead bodily"* (Colossians 2:9-10). Jesus was saying we would come out from under the old ways of Israel, symbolized by the fig tree, connect with the true Tree of Life, Jesus Christ, and, through Him, be carriers of the Promised Land of the Kingdom of God.

In our ministry together, Adrian Beale and I always engage in the intimacy of worship and praying in the spirit before we operate in the gifts. An intimate relationship with the Lord brings an understanding of our identity in Christ and enables us to carry the glory in worship, all of which activates the angelic realm. We line up with the cascade of angelic presence—angels ascending and descending. What we are doing is aligning with the angelic realm so that heaven invades the space, whether it is in a business meeting, a time of ministry, a courtroom, or standing before rulers and politicians.

Becoming Receptive to Heavenly Encounters

The importance of separating truth from fantasy is one of the reasons why I teach that your imagination is a very important part of your devotions. Task-oriented prayer has its place, but I believe it is important to ascend into a higher realm with the Lord where we can wrap our imagination around the promises of God in Scripture. In Psalm 1:2-3, we read that the person who delights to meditate in the Word of God is like a tree planted beside a stream, able to bear fruit even in a time of famine. When we allow our imagination to give us a mental picture of that tree and its source of nourishment, we grasp the true depths of its meaning. We will be fruitless unless we are watered by intimacy with God's Word.

The sanctified imagination is a facet of scriptural meditation; and as such, it is essential for a heart-understanding of the written Word. This is particularly so with the prophetic books such as Revelation and Ezekiel. Using your God-given imagination to assimilate the Kingdom of God will bring revelation of the promises, the true scroll of the eternal Word of the Lord. As we meditate on the Word, we come into the place of thanksgiving and go through the gates into the courts of praise (Psalm 100). This is how we become receptive to heavenly encounters.

God requires that we be led by the Spirit, *"For those who are led by the Spirit of God are the children of God"* (Romans 8:14 New International Version). Sons and daughters walk in the authority to govern the Kingdom on earth even as it is governed in Heaven. Daniel was one who walked in this authority, and the Babylonian kings, Nebuchadnezzar and Belshazzar, honored him for it. They respected his wisdom and integrity. Through being led by the Spirit of God, Daniel brought those proud and powerful men to humble themselves before God. Daniel is a prototype of those who will move in supernatural power to influence leaders and rulers in the days of darkness to come.

Daniel prophesied that knowledge and understanding would be *"sealed up"* until the *"time of the end,"* but he went on to reveal that when it is time for that unsealing, there would be an unprecedented *"increase of knowledge"* upon the earth (Daniel 12). I believe this explosion of knowledge will take place within the next ten to twenty years. With this volcano of technical know-how, satan will use technology to counterfeit supernatural power and bring great deception. This counterfeit power will have the effect of desensitizing people to the signs and wonders demonstrated by God's people, His Church.

However, the raising up of the Elijahs will bring an increase of Daniel-type wisdom which cannot be counterfeited. King Nebuchadnezzar in Babylon and Pharaoh in Egypt, were quick to recognize that Daniel and Joseph were wiser than any of their own enchanters, magicians, and educated men. In the same way, today's world rulers will come to acknowledge the superior wisdom of Jesus Christ. God's wisdom not only springs from righteousness, it is supernatural and demands attention. When wisdom from above is demonstrated, it reveals the true saints of God and brings a clear separation between real and false wonders. God's true power is undeniable.

It is imperative that the Body of Christ be led by the Spirit to embrace the revelation of God's Kingdom. With the increase of technology in this age of artificial intelligence, Christians who are of the flesh will have no substance and no power as agents for spiritual change—but those who tap into the Gate of Kingdom revelation will see the presence of God released. The cleverness of advanced technology will convince many people that they are seeing miracles, they may even credit them as coming from God. The enemy of our souls can and will exploit that, but he will never be able to imitate the presence and the love of God. As the saying has it—God doesn't *have* love, He *is* love. The eternal reality of that is beyond our comprehension, but we can tap into it by faith and release it into the natural atmosphere. As we do that, people will respond to His love even in this end-age of *"many shall run to and fro, and knowledge shall increase"* (Daniel 12:4).

When the Body of Christ calls Kingdom signs and wonders from the invisible realms into the physical and changes the spiritual atmosphere of the natural realms, people will respond to God's presence as never before. Truly, Jesus is the Gate, the Way, the Truth, the Life. He is the prototype of how we are to walk as men and women anointed and filled with the Holy Spirit. Yes, even as the only begotten Son of God, the prophesied Messiah, He is the model of what we are to be: *"He who says he abides in Him ought himself also to walk just as He walked"* (1 John 2:6). If we claim to know Jesus, then we must walk the way He walked. That's not about religious works, it's about living in the revelation that it was God's intention that we do everything Jesus did, and in the way He did it; that is, in love and the power of God's presence.

In the heavenly encounter I had in Hong Kong when I stood on the edge of heaven listening to wave after wave of glorious sound, everything, even the plant life, was worshipping the Lord. Then I heard the waves of sound change to a melody I recognized. A magnificent male voice began to sing, "I could sing of Your love forever." I was moved to tears and was overcome by the awesomeness of the sound of God's love. And even as I was thinking, *I know that song,* the Spirit of God said to me, "That song already existed in heaven before it came to earth." Immediately, I understood that it was born in the heavenly realms before it was formed in the heart of the composer. That type of worship is integral to changing the spiritual atmosphere. You can tell the difference in a church meeting when a worship leader taps into eternal realms and goes through the Gate in the spirit. The intimacy that leader has with God overflows so that worship goes beyond a song service to a higher level of adoration.

Remember what Jesus told the woman at the well. You don't have to go the mountain anymore. You can worship in spirit and truth and go straight into His presence, wherever you may be located physically. In this New Covenant era, we are privileged to be gates and also carriers of The Gate, because Jesus lives in us. As we worship, we pull the presence of God into the natural realm and alter the spiritual frequency in that locality. It is in that changed atmosphere that the genius mind of God is released to us, so that we can receive inventions, songs, art, and also business wisdom. We are enabled to receive solutions to all manner of problems, just like Joseph and Daniel experienced.

God's People to Represent His Government

This is the time for God's people to shine, to represent the heavenly, eternal government of God. This is a time for God's people to position themselves in places of influence and to actually demonstrate the rulership of Christ. New covenant believers need to grasp this as a revelation. When we come to a place of intimacy with God, it is through the gate of worship in spirit and truth, so that the Kingdom of God will manifest on earth as it is in heaven with angels ascending and descending around us. In this changed atmosphere sinners come to repentance and revival takes place.

What does it mean to worship in spirit and truth? Our God is invisible to the naked eye, so any worship we offer Him is by faith in the spirit realm. Truth, on the other hand, relates to the genuine wholehearted nature of that worship. To worship in spirit and truth speaks of a heart-directed act of faith using our sanctified imagination to exult the King of Glory, wherever we happen to be.

An incident in the Old Testament is a dramatic illustration of this. A company of prophets playing musical instruments came down from a high place to meet Saul, the newly anointed king. The prophets knew their worship would produce a spiritual atmosphere in which Saul could receive an impartation to rule effectively. They understood they had authority to praise everywhere, not exclusively in the tent of the tabernacle, and they knew their worship opened a heavenly gate. I believe that they tapped into the realm of angels ascending and descending that Jesus spoke of in John 1:51. Scripture records that Saul was transformed into a different man as a result of meeting the worshipping prophets (1 Samuel 10:5-11). *"When they came to the hill there, behold, a group of prophets met him; and the*

Spirit of God came upon him mightily, so that he prophesied among them" (1 Samuel 10:10 NASB).

In the New Testament, we see Jesus bringing this revelation to everyone. He taught that worship is actually in spirit and in truth and is not dependent on a specific location. All believers may access the presence of God in spirit and in truth and bring heaven to earth. In this way the very King of Glory manifests in and through His people.

As the eternal Kingdom is revealed and demonstrated by the new breed, there will be displays of power even to the magnitude of interacting with angels to wage heavenly war with principalities and powers. And, just as in the days of Daniel and Nebuchadnezzar, present-day leaders in government will also be influenced to the point of repenting and giving glory to the Most High God.

Be Refreshed Continually

As an itinerant minister, I travel and minister internationally. The schedules are tight, with little to no downtime between meetings. Several years ago traveling and carrying pastoral responsibilities took its toll, leaving me feeling exhausted. For those in ministry, it is wise to be aware of the warning signs of doing too much in your own strength. Exhaustion and burnout may cause you to stop caring about your role. It may also cause personal issues to arise in your life and make you susceptible to a moral fall. It is imperative to remain intimate with the Lord, take breaks, and even have sabbaticals. It is important to be refreshed continually. The Lord often uses angels to warn me about my level of exhaustion.

Here is an example: After one particular tour, I arrived home feeling completely exhausted, but I couldn't take a break because I was to take on the governmental role within my home church and conduct the meetings while the senior leader was hosting a crusade overseas. As I drove to a meeting, a ladybug (also known as a ladybird) appeared inside the car. It attracted my attention because I hadn't seen one since I was a child and I thought it odd that it should appear in my car. I watched it walking up and down my left thigh and that also seemed quite strange. At that point the Lord's Spirit spoke to me, "Adam, what do you see? This is a sign. I have sent an angel to strengthen you."

In the natural, ladybugs protect fruit from aphids that try to destroy a plant's fruitfulness. In other words, ladybugs preserve the fruit. The left thigh is symbolic of natural physical strength and health. By drawing my attention to the ladybug walking up and down my thigh, the Lord was showing me that He was strengthening me physically in the natural realm and equipping me to have a sound mind. He was protecting me from having my fruit destroyed.

What Do You See?

The Lord speaks to us all the time through prophetic symbols and metaphors. He sends angels to direct our attention to those signs. Sometimes He will communicate through a thought that comes as a question; at other times He will use images and signs in the natural world to gain our attention and deliver His message. A good example is the prophet Jeremiah. The Lord often spoke to Jeremiah by asking him what he saw in the physical or natural realm. Jeremiah may well have been walking in the market place when the Lord asked him:

> *"What do you see, Jeremiah?" And I said, "I see a rod of an almond tree." Then the Lord said to me, "You have seen well, for I am watching over My word to perform it." The word of the Lord came to me a second time saying, "What do you see?" And I said, "I see a boiling pot, facing away from the north." Then the Lord said to me, "Out of the north the evil will break forth on all the inhabitants of the land"* (Jeremiah 1:11-14 NASB).

The chapter goes on to describe the northern armies that will be used as instruments of judgment against Judah for its idolatry. As Jeremiah's attention was drawn to the sign or natural incident, he would receive a revelation of what God was saying through it, and from that he would prophesy the word of the Lord.

On another occasion, God instructed Jeremiah to visit the potter. Upon seeing the potter at work, he heard what God was saying to Israel:

> *"Arise and go down to the potter's house, and there I will cause you to hear My words." Then I went down to the potter's house, and there he was, making something at the wheel. And the vessel that he made of clay was marred in the hand of the potter; so he made it again into another vessel, as it seemed good to the potter to make. Then the word of the Lord came to me, saying: "O house of Israel, can I not do with you as this potter?" says the Lord. "Look, as the clay is in the potter's hand, so are you in My hand, O house of Israel!"* (Jeremiah 18:2-6)

The Lord went on to instruct Jeremiah to speak to the people about repentance in an attempt to save them from the coming judgment. I believe the Lord spoke to Jeremiah through these natural incidents so that Jeremiah could prophetically warn the people in as graphic a way as possible.

Summary

- Angels are activated to serve when we worship God.

- There are gates opened into other spiritual realms through trauma, fear, horror, and abuse.

- By activating a gate of deception, Jacob invited a curse upon his life.

- Jesus is the only true Gate of entrance to God and the eternal realm.

- We line up with angels—ascending and descending—when we worship.

- Through worship we are allowing angels to invade whatever environment where we are—work, business, courtroom, home, etc.

- When we wrap our imagination around the promises of God, we bear fruit.

- Using your God-given sanctified imagination by meditating on Scripture will bring revelation so that the promises of God manifest.

- Daniel is a prototype of believers who will move in supernatural power to influence world leaders in the days to come.

- Technical know-how will be used by satan to counterfeit God's power and will lead many into deception.

- When wisdom from above is demonstrated it reveals the true sons of God and will bring a clear separation between true and false wonders.

- Only those led by the Spirit will tap into the Gate of Kingdom revelation, others will have no substance and power.

- True signs and wonders will see people respond to God's presence like never before.

- Jesus is the ultimate Prototype and we are to walk as He walked (1 John 2:6).

- Now is the time for us to take up our spiritual governmental role.

- Saul's meeting of prophets in worship is a powerful illustration of the impartation that takes place in worship.

- It is important to take time out with God.

- The ladybug illustration is a demonstration that God can and does use the natural realm to communicate angelic intervention.

- God will often communicate by asking a question, as He did with Jeremiah.

CHAPTER 11

UNSEEN ANGELS

Adrian Beale

Why a Dictionary?

Why is there a dictionary in a book about angels? That is a good question. As spirit beings whose primary domain is beyond our own, very much angelic activity goes unnoticed. For the most part, angels are the anonymous servants of the King of Glory, and as good servants theirs is to do their work efficiently without drawing attention to themselves. Having said that, however, their exploits and interventions on earth often provide a fingerprint of their handiwork. While these clues to angelic activity can be encouraging and faith-building, there must be reasons why more often than not their activity remains hidden from the natural human being. One key reason why much is not shown openly has to do with who is credited by their intermediary acts.

The bottom line is that humankind has a propensity to idolatry. While in the Western world that may not be stone carvings on a mantel shelf, we may nonetheless display a common heart when we are consumed with money, position, sports, material things, and notoriety that equally fill our time and focus. So given that we are all tarred with the same brush in having this innate disposition, God has chosen to keep most angelic activity veiled so that the spiritually immature are not drawn aside into error and deceived from the truth.

With angelic activity in mind, another example of Western idolatry may be going to church with a focus to find feathers, gemstones, oil, or manna. That, by the way, is a mark of spiritual immaturity. However, if those signs follow the preaching of the Word and we are there to glorify God, then these appearances witness angelic activity and an impartation strengthening faith for the miraculous.

Open Versus Hidden Angelic Involvement

Let's consider a couple of biblical examples to open and explore this topic. First, when Jesus was resurrected, the Scriptures record that an earthquake marked the coming of an angel to move the stone from His sepulcher:

> *And behold, there was a great earthquake; for an angel of the Lord descended from heaven, and came and rolled back the stone from the door, and sat on it* (Matthew 28:2).

The angel was seen by the two women who came to visit the tomb, and the guards who were set to secure the stone. To the believers, the angel's appearance not only was a display of power, it brought renewed hope and great joy; while on the other hand, the soldiers were overcome with fear and trepidation (Matthew 28:1-8). On this occasion, the manifestation of the angel declared and brought assurance of Christ's resurrection, removed any question of foul play, and at the same time disarmed those who were employed to obstruct the purposes of God.

That scene was not unlike one experienced by the apostle Paul when he and Silas were imprisoned at Philippi, only without the appearance of an angel. On that occasion they were incarcerated after casting out a demon from a fortune-teller (Acts 16:16-24). Their release was also accompanied by an earthquake; and if you take time to consider the scene, it is likely it was also at the hand of angels. In fact, before this episode, the book of Acts presents a repeated theme of angels delivering believers from prison (Acts 5:19-25; 12:7-19).

When considered more closely, it is noted that Paul and Silas had an audience of unbelieving prisoners who not only witnessed their imprisonment but also their prayer and praise (Acts 16:24-25). The Bible records that the earthquake was sudden and powerful, suggesting its supernatural origin. Actually, it was so powerful that it shook the very foundations of the prison, to the point where *"all the doors were opened and everyone's chains were loosed"* (Acts 16:26).

Given that this incident led to the salvation of the jailer and his family (Acts 16:34), what do you think would have happened if an angel or two were shown to be the agents that brought the prisoners' release? Remember, this is a Roman colony of Greek decent with Athens as its capital, which provoked Paul's spirit because it was fully given over to idols (Acts 18:16). Surely, we would have to acknowledge that the opportunity to plant the church on the Gospel at Philippi would have been compromised. Adding weight to the likelihood of angelic intervention was the fact that Paul and Silas were worshipping in song at the moment of release. Worship is a virtual invitation for angels (Psalm 69:34; 148:2; 150:6; Revelation 5:8-13).

Angelic Protection

Angels are all around us and one of their primary roles is the protection of innocent children and the saints. Though most of us don't even give it a second thought, many people have experienced incidents where they were miraculously protected. Some have been delayed on their journey only to find five minutes down the track a major accident with automobile parts strewn across the road. A friend recently related that he was riding home from work on his bicycle and barely missed being wiped out by a car as it scraped his front wheel.

A number of others can recount being cut out of a wreck while having paramedics or police officers say, "Looking at this mess, there is no way you should even be alive!" And there are yet others who for some unexplainable reason chose to change their routine, like going to lunch early, only to find when they returned to work there had been a major incident while they were gone. One thing is for sure, those who survive major catastrophic incidents are protected because they have a call of God on their lives to make a difference in our world. God is not the author of whatever took place but He will use the incident to awaken us to our destiny scroll.

Things Lining Up

Have there been times in your life when things miraculously lined up or fell into place? I can recall a time when my wife and I were seeking direction where there were more than ten signs that miraculously lined up. Though we didn't recognize it at the time, in hindsight, we would now have to acknowledge that angels had to have been orchestrating things behind the scenes. There was a confirmatory street sign, a ship's name, a tourist brochure, three independent Scriptures, an unexpected phone call, a timely visiting speaker's Sunday morning message, and a forced house move all lining up to confirm a major move. In this case I believe there were so many elements because the decision we had to make went against peer assessment and our own personal inclinations.

When Abraham sent his servant to find a wife for his son, Isaac, he assured him God would send an angel before him to prosper his way (Genesis 24:7). When the servant arrived at his destination, he offered up a specific prayer to speed and qualify God's selection:

> *Then he said, "O Lord God of my master Abraham, please give me success this day, and show kindness to my master Abraham. Behold, here I stand by the well of water, and the daughters of the men of the city are coming out to draw water. Now let it be that the young woman to whom I say, 'Please let down your pitcher that I may drink,' and she says, 'Drink, and I will also give your camels a drink'—let her be the one You have appointed for Your servant Isaac. And by this I will know that You have shown kindness to my master." And it happened, before he had finished speaking,*

that behold, Rebekah, who was born to Bethuel, son of Milcah, the wife of Nahor, Abraham's brother, came out with her pitcher on her shoulder (Genesis 24:12-15).

Notice that the servant didn't pray to the angel, he rightly brought his petition to God. What caused Rebekah to be the first on the scene? Was she customarily punctual or was she internally prompted to be early that day? You get the impression that her desire to go the extra mile and draw water for the camels came as a possible afterthought, because unlike the prayer it came with a hiatus after serving him:

So she said, "Drink, my lord." Then she quickly let her pitcher down to her hand, and gave him a drink. And when she had finished giving him a drink, she said, "I will draw water for your camels also, until they have finished drinking" (Genesis 24:18-19).

Did God intervene and have the angel soften her heart to extend such hospitality? Regardless of the answer, even after these two apparent green lights, Abraham's servant demonstrated wisdom in waiting for confirmation:

And the man, wondering at her, remained silent as to know whether the Lord had made his journey prosperous or not (Genesis 24:21).

It was only after a further exchange had taken place that firmly established Rebekah's heritage that the servant bowed, worshipped, and publicly acknowledged God's hand in successfully leading him. While the angel does receive a mention in the servant recounting his testimony (Genesis 24:40), he makes no appearance and it is God who is credited with the successful outcome (Genesis 24:48).

What Part Do Angels Play in Bringing the Unsaved to Christ?

Considering this incident in Genesis 24, on another level Isaac is a picture of Christ. His Father—God the Father—has sent forth an unnamed servant (the Holy Spirit) to woo an uncircumcised (Gentile) bride (the Church), based on the testimony of the servant, a display of the gifts, and the unseen working of angels. This means angelic assistance is to be expected, particularly when we are about our Father's business and the growth and welfare of the Church is at hand.

What part do angels play in bringing the unsaved out of the world? (See Numbers 20:16; Hebrews 1:14.) The assistance given to Abraham's servant in his quest to find Isaac's bride would suggest angels arrange the timing of any salvation rendezvous. On another occasion, an angel directed Philip to go down the road from Jerusalem to Gaza, a journey that led to a court official's salvation (Acts 8:26-39). Was the angel also responsible for any other part of the Ethiopian eunuch making a confession of belief in Jesus Christ? Did he also influence the Ethiopian eunuch to be reading Isaiah 53 at the exact moment Philip encountered him? It is highly likely. What we can say is angels are critical assistants in getting the message, through sons and daughters, to thirsting souls.

Who Gathered the Animals for Noah?

How are angels involved when it comes to crusades and mass salvations? Angels are recorded as being involved in bringing Israel out of Egypt, *"When we cried out to the Lord, He heard our voice and sent the Angel and brought us up out of Egypt..."* (Numbers 20:16). And angels continue to play their part for the heirs of salvation today (Hebrews 1:14).

Given that the Gentiles were depicted as unclean animals in Peter's vision on the rooftop (Acts 10:10-16), if we further acknowledge the parallel of our journey out of the world with Israel's out of Egypt and link each with Noah's forerunning narrative of building the ark, we can answer the question, "Who gathered the animals for Noah?"

> *And of every living thing of all flesh, two of every sort shall you bring into the ark, to keep them alive with you; they shall be male and female. Of the birds after their kind, of animals after their kind, and of every creeping thing of the earth after its kind, two of every kind will come to you to keep them alive* (Genesis 6:19-20).

By extrapolation, it seems pretty straight forward that angels gathered the animals for Noah. This means angels are employed to gather the lost and bring them to crusades to hear about and enter into salvation through Christ, the Door.

Parents Naming Their Children

Before the birth of John the Baptist, Zacharias, his father, was visited by an angel who not only brought news of John's future birth but also his name, *"But the angel said to him, 'Do not be afraid, Zacharias, for your prayer is heard; and your wife Elisabeth will bear you a son, and you shall call his name John'"* (Luke 1:13).

Mary, who was engaged to Joseph, received a similar visitation from the angel Gabriel and was greeted with a comparable announcement, *"And behold, you will conceive in your womb and bring forth a Son, and shall call His name JESUS"* (Luke 1:31).

These accounts record that both families received angelic visitations to announce supernatural conception and the naming of their child. In each of these cases both the conception and the naming of the child was contrary to family expectation (Luke 1:60-63; 2:21). And even though these two pregnancies were initially questioned, as being beyond human comprehension, the Scriptures paint the picture that no birth takes place without God knowing, fashioning, and having a script for the individual's life. Indeed, God strengthened Jeremiah by confirming his calling and destiny from the womb as well, *"Before I formed you in the womb I knew you; before you were born I sanctified you; I ordained you a prophet to the nations"* (Jeremiah 1:5).

King David gave voice to similar understanding when he penned:

> *For You formed my inward parts; You covered me in my mother's womb. I will praise You, for I am fearfully and wonderfully made; marvelous are Your works, and that my soul knows very well. My frame was not hidden from You, when I was made in secret, and skillfully wrought in the lowest parts of the earth. Your eyes saw my substance, being yet unformed. And in Your book they all were written, the days fashioned for me, when as yet there were none of them* (Psalm 139:13-16).

In a world where so many people are confused about their own identity, given that most angelic activity is deliberately veiled and goes unnoticed, could it be that God had angels "seed" a parent's thoughts about the name of their child before birth? Even if they didn't acknowledge it, this would mean that rather than just providing a label, because identity is the foundation of destiny like a strand of DNA, in naming you your parents encoded your unique calling and destiny. Every one of us is more than happenstance, and I believe angels were as much a part of our entry into the world as they were for John and Jesus. Our part is to have confidence in God's handiwork and seek Him to open the scroll—for in knowing Him we walk out what is written in our destiny.

One-Time Appearances

While penning material for this book, I had opportunity to catch a few scenes from a movie I had watched previously on a flight overseas. The movie is titled *The Walk,* and is about Philippe Petit, a French high-wire performer who walked between the Twin Towers of the World Trade Center in New York in 1974. There is one scene, as Philippe is about to do the walk where a stranger dressed in a suit comes up onto the rooftop. In the movie, it is like all the work of getting to this point is in jeopardy of being lost. However, nothing is said between Philippe and this well-dressed intruder who silently looks at the high-wire stretched between the buildings and back at Philippe a couple of times. The stranger then walks back down the stairs from the rooftop and according to Philippe, is never seen again. It was the silence they shared—like Samson's father's encounter when *"the Angel of the Lord appeared no more"* (Judges 13:21)—that tells us this was an angel sent to protect the high-wire artist.

I raise this illustration for you to recall times when a person suddenly appears at a critical juncture in your life and just as easily is gone and never reappears. These are God's servants—angels—intervening in your life to protect you through a potential hazard that threatens the call on your life. I can't help but wonder what message God was conveying through this world famous event where a high wire was stretched between the north and south towers?

There was an event where an angel appeared and then disappeared when Adam and I were ministering at a church in Sydney. Adam was in the process of announcing an opportunity to sow into our ministry when a teenage girl came up to him at the podium and interrupted what he was saying to bring a message to him. She said a really simple thing, "God is pleased with what you are doing!" She then laid hands on him and he fell down in the power of the Spirit in the middle of the offering. When he eventually got up, the impartation he received caused him to say, "Did anyone get the number of that truck!"

It was a very special night for a number of reasons, the fire of God kept people in the prayer line even though so much rain fell that night that cars were being flooded in the parking lot. The thing about this girl's appearance was—no one knew who she was, no one saw her come into the building, and no one saw her leave! I found out later that Adam had spoken to God, questioning his call to ministry before we were taken to the church that evening.

Summary

- Angels are anonymous servants of the King of Glory; theirs is to do their job without drawing attention to themselves.

- Angels often leave fingerprints of their handiwork.

- Why are there not more open sightings of angels? So we don't idolize them.

- Paul and Silas' release from prison is an example of hidden angelic intervention.

- Angels protect children and the saints—believers in Jesus Christ.

- When things line up or miraculously fall into place, it is likely that angels are involved.

- Abraham's servant did not pray to the angel that accompanied him.

- Abraham's servant displayed wisdom in waiting for confirmation that Rebekah was Isaac's chosen bride.

- Angels arrange the timing of salvation rendezvous.

- Angels will assist in getting the message of salvation to thirsty souls.

- Angels gathered the animals for Noah.

- No birth takes place without God knowing and fashioning a destiny scroll for that individual.

- Angels "seed" every child's name to a parent, and in doing so encode their identity and destiny.

- Strangers you see one time at critical junctures in your life are likely angels.

CHAPTER 12

FINAL THOUGHTS

Adrian Beale

Telegraphed Activity

We may engage angels in dreams (Matthew 1:20; 2:13,19) and visions (Acts 10:3) as key revelatory interfaces between heaven and earth. As Adam has shared, they may also be personally encountered in everyday life (Judges 6:11-12; 13:3). Given that much of the time their work is covert and hidden behind the scenes, most of their handiwork goes unnoticed were it not for earthly evidence communicating their activity. Just as an ocean will reflect the sky above it, heavenly activity is often mirrored and telegraphed metaphorically by incidents on earth.

Witness of the Presence

Not only may angels bring a godly presence into a room, often when people are retelling their angelic encounters there will be the witness of that same glory presence. After all, if Moses' face reflected the glory of God because of his audience with Yahweh (Exodus 34:29-30,35), it is not unreasonable to expect that angels, who abide in God's presence, will also bear that same glory. This is certainly one indicator of the truth of a person's testimony of angels.

Unusual Animal Behavior

It is not unusual for animals to display uncharacteristic behavior in the presence of spirit beings. Have you ever seen a cat suddenly hiss and arch its back for no apparent reason? In some situations, like Balaam's donkey, it will be seeing or sensing something beyond this realm (Numbers 22:22-34).

In this type of situation, or for that matter any sensed angelic activity, your task is to discern whether what is happening is positive (godly) or negative (evil). This is done by assessing the context of the event. How do you assess context? By asking the following questions:

- Who had the experience?

- What happened?

- Where were they?

- When did it take place?

- How did they feel? (This is always a key question.)

- Why would God give such an dream, vision, event, or encounter to this person?

Answering these questions will also give you understanding of the possible purpose of such an angelic intervention and/or interaction.

The Blood

If there is evidence of the demonic or fallen angels, it is important that the location and heart of the believers present be "covered" in the blood of Jesus Christ. The blood, when understood, is so powerful that it presents a barrier over which destructive and evil spirits cannot enter.

Adam and I are on tour often, which means we regularly sleep in hotels that at times are used for ungodly activities. In these situations we pray the covering of the blood of Christ over the room and over our hearts, that nothing ungodly is able to cross either threshold.

Refer to Scripture

The Scriptures are our standard for faith and practice. This means that our primary reference needs to be the Bible. If possible, look at the angelic encounter through the lens of Scripture. The dictionary included in the back of this book has scriptural links for you to look up for most entries. Do any of these or their links relate to your circumstances? If there is no listing in the dictionary, also consider where in the Bible there is mention of similar or parallel incidences.

If there is a scriptural precedent, consider what God was doing or saying through the angelic intervention. What was the person doing with whom the angel had interaction? If the angel or angels were unseen, why were they unseen? What did they do?

We have often found that an event may not have a scriptural example, like Adam's ladybug incident. In that case you need to consider the characteristics, role, or nature of the particular insect, bird, plant, fish, etc. involved by doing a little research. In digging deeper to find information, you will likely open new levels of understanding that unlock the meaning of the incident that gained your attention. Do not rush to conclusions, it is always better to come away from an encounter and take stock and wisely weigh its purpose before launching into a presumptuous assessment.

Two-Verse Entries

At times the entries in the dictionary will contain two verses in parentheses. Examples:

Imaginary Friend: (1) (Matthew 18:10 and Daniel 10:7,11).

In this situation, to understand how an angel could manifest as an imaginary friend, you need to combine the two verses. Looking at Matthew 18:10 we see that children have guardian angels, and by referring to Daniel 10:7 we discover that others did not see Daniel's angel. A person blind to spiritual things could easily underplay the encounter by saying that Daniel had seen an imaginary friend.

Similarly, another example is found under Hawk:

Hawk: (1) Good: Angel destroying poverty spirit (pigeon/s) (Malachi 3:11 [note: Lord of hosts] and Leviticus 5:7).

Here God is referred to as the *Lord of hosts,* suggesting that angels are involved in His intervention in rebuking the devourer. When we combine this with an understanding that a poor person's offering was two turtledoves or pigeons from Leviticus 5:7, we can see that a poverty spirit may be represented by one or two pigeons. As hawks often prey on other birds, a scene where a hawk takes out a pigeon (if associated with a good feeling) possibly depicts God's angel taking out the poverty spirit.

For Mature Believers

Whether angels appear in a dream, vision, or their presence is conveyed through an earthly incident, the dictionary that follows is provided to not only help recognize their involvement but also link Scriptures that may suggest the possible purpose for such interventions. This is by no means exhaustive and is to encourage and strengthen maturing believers who endeavor to keep Jesus in the forefront of their spiritual expression.

Please understand that the dictionary in this book is about angelic activity only. For the understanding of other elements, please refer to the books: *The Divinity Code to Understanding Your Dreams* and *Visions* or *God's Prophetic Symbolism in Everyday Life*.

Caution

If we are at any time engaging angels or wanting to interpret their activity, the Scriptures provide repeated warnings about taking onboard anything that is not in line with the Gospel of Jesus Christ as presented throughout the recognized canon of Scripture. *This area is so open to deception that we must stress the material set forth in this book and dictionary is presented for emotionally balanced and mature believers who are walking in accordance with sound biblical teaching and who are accountable to recognized Spirit-filled oversight.* We are called to *test* the spirits because there are many false prophets who openly leverage their spiritual encounters to assert their apostleship and lead people astray (1 John 4:1).

According to Scripture, the marks of a false prophet are that they will do one or more of the following:

- Preach another Jesus (2 Corinthians 11:4; Colossians 2:19)

- Preach another Gospel (Galatians 1:8)

- Preach another Spirit (2 Corinthians 11:4)

- Isolate believers by drawing them to themselves (2 Corinthians 11:13-15; Colossians 2:19)

- Boast of their encounters while not embracing Christ as Head of the Church (Colossians 2:18-19)

- Worship angels (Colossians 2:18)

Judge All Angelic Interaction

The importance of judging what is communicated in angelic interventions cannot be overstated. This takes into account that we deliver God's treasure through earthen vessels and also acknowledges that none of us has arrived yet. We are all in the process of growing in the things of the Spirit. While it can be tempting to leverage your spirituality by openly sharing your angelic encounters, sometimes it is best to be like Mary, who held her experience in her heart (Luke 2:19). On other occasions, like the apostle Paul we may need to share that an angel of God was in our midst to encourage the others going through a storm (Acts 27:23).

As with all prophetic revelation, what, if anything, is conveyed by an angel needs to be judged and evaluated. When doing so, you might consider the following questions:

- Is it in line with Scripture?

- If what is being said is corrective, is it free of condemnation?

- Does the message carried provide a future and a hope?

- Is there an inner witness or conviction that what is being said is truth?

- Does the word and/or experience meet a heart need?

- Does what is being said line up with what God has been saying through other avenues of guidance?

A negative response to one of these puts what is being said in question. At the very least, it should cause us to put the encounter on the shelf until confirmation is received. A negative response to two or more of these questions seriously puts the communication in doubt. If there is uncertainty, there is nothing wrong with asking God for confirmation like Manoah, Samson's father (Judges 13:8-9).

Note: We never pray to angels, we always pray and lift our petitions to God. The authors take no responsibility for poor decisions based on misinterpretation of material presented.

Summary

- Just as an ocean reflects the sky above it, heavenly activity is often mirrored and telegraphed metaphorically by incidents on earth.

- When people talk about angelic encounters, there is often a witness of the glory.

- Animals may display unusual behavior in the presence of spirit beings.

- Assess context to determine whether spirit activity is evil or elect in nature.

- Cover yourself with prayer in the blood of Christ when in foreign bedrooms.

- Look at all angelic activity through the lens of Scripture.

- Scripture is our primary reference for the interpretation of any suspected angelic activity.

- For incidents involving elements outside the vocabulary of Scripture, research to gain understanding of the characteristics of any plant, animal, insect, fish, etc.

- Take your time in declaring the purpose of any angelic intervention.

- This book is for mature believers walking in accordance with sound biblical teaching and who are accountable to recognized Spirit-filled oversight.

- Test the spirits because there are many false prophets.

- Review the characteristics of false prophets.

- There are times to share openly and times to keep silent about angelic interventions.

- Judge all angelic communication according to the guidelines stated.

ANGEL DICTIONARY

A

Abaddon: See *Angel of Death*

Accuser: (1) Devil/satan; (2) One of his minions
(1) Job 1:6-9; Revelation 12:10.

Adjustment Bureau: (1) Destiny Angel/s; (2) Angels of intervention
(1-2) Matthew 1:20-21; Acts 8:26; 11:13

Alcohol Testing (Booze bus cop): (1) Angels of separation
(1) Matthew 13:49-50 (separating the righteous from the unrighteous)
  See *Road Block* and *Stop Sign*

Airforce: (1) Heavenly host/army
(1) Matthew 16:27; 25:31; 2 Thessalonians 1:7; Revelation 8:13; 12;7

Alarm Clock: See *Wake-Up Call*

Alignment (things lining up/falling into place): (1) Advance guard angel; (2) Guiding angel
(1-2) Genesis 24:7,14-15,40.
  See *Billboard, Lookout,* and *Sign/Sign writer (sign reading Alignment)*

Amber: (1) Glorious angel/s; (2) Angel from His presence
(1) Ezekiel 1:4-5,27; 8:2; (2) Luke 2:9; Luke 1:19; and Jude 1:24.
  See *Glory*

Angel of Death: (1) Luke 16:22; Acts 12:23; Revelation 9:11
  See *Grim Reaper, Locust; Spirit of Death* and *Undertaker*

Animal Behavior (Unusual or out of character): (1) Unseen angelic activity seen by animals
(1) Numbers 22:23,25,30

Anorexia: See *Spirit of Death*

Apollyon: See *Angel of Death*

Archway: (1) Angelic portal; (2) Angelic covering/protection
(1-2) Genesis 28:12; Exodus 25:18-20; John 1:51

Ariel: (1) Lion of God; (2) May be associated with Jerusalem.
(1) Jewish Traditional reference to a class of angels (Isaiah 33:7)

Army: (1) God's heavenly army/host
(1) 2 Samuel 5:24; Matthew 26:53; Revelation 12:7
   See *Soldier*

Army Camp: (1) A camp or garrison of angels (speaks of
protection/potential intervention)
(1) Genesis 32:1-2

Assistant (often unseen): (1) Angelic assistance; (2) Someone
assisting you in a dream
(1) Consider that Abraham's servant had an angel assist him but
remained unseen. (Genesis 24:7, 40); (2) 1 Kings 19:5; Matthew 1:20

Au Pair: (1) Guardian angel; (2) Assigned personal angel
(1) Matthew 18:10.
See *Baby Sitter* and *Nanny*

Aura: (atmosphere emanating from a person, place, or thing):
(1) Atmosphere associated with angelic activity; (2) Warning of
deceiving angel (when you feel uneasy)
(1) Judges 13:6; Ezekiel 1:13; Revelation 10:1; (2) 2 Corinthians 11:14

Azazel: (1) Desert region; (2) Fallen angel; (3) Spirit of lust; (4) Seduces into sinful practice; (5) Immature handling of knowledge (that brings sorrow)

(1) Leviticus 16:8; (2-5) 1 Enoch 7-8; Genesis 6:1-4; Ecclesiastes 1:18

B

Babysitter: (1) Guardian angel

(1) Matthew 18:10.
 See *Au Pair* and *Nanny*

Barachiel: (1) Lightning of God

(1) Zechariah 9:14; Matthew 24:27; Revelation 4:5-6

Barrenness: (1) Angel/s about to announce conception (when feelings of strength follow encounter)

(1) Judges 13:3; Luke 1:13; Luke 1:31

Battle/s: (1) Angels undertaking spiritual warfare (if you are under attack or see a battle taking place)

(1) Jude 9; 2 Kings 19:35; Daniel 10:13
 See *Dogfight (Aerial)* and *Marching*

Bee/s: (1) Revelatory angels; (2) Harvest angels

(1) Genesis 28:12; 1 Samuel 14:27; Ephesians 1:18; (2) Matthew 24:31; Revelation 14:15

Beryl: (1) Stone/color associated with spirit activity; (2) Strength, stability

(1) Ezekiel 1:16; (2) Revelation 21:19

Billboard (Elevated Sign): (1) Heavenly guidance/direction; (2) Sign

(1-2) Luke 2:9-14; 1 Chronicles 21:16 (where the sword represents the word)
 See *Alignment, Sign / Sign writer*

Binoculars: (1) Watcher angel/s (fallen and elect); (2) Future prophetic decree (seeing in the distance/horizon)

(1) Daniel 4:13; 23; (2) Luke 1:32. See the book of Enoch

Bird/s: (1) Angel or angelic host; (2) Birds in a tree (angels drawn to people)

(1) Luke 2:13-14 (Flock); (2) Matthew 13:32 & Psalm 1:1-3 (birds = angels, trees = person)

  See *Cockatoo/s, Eagle,* and *Feathers*

Blinded (unable to see/be seen): (1) Veiled angel/s; (2) Physically blind person, an angel may be displaying a person's spiritual state; (3) Angel of judgment

(1) 2 Kings 6:17 (angels there but couldn't see them); (2-3) Genesis 19:11 (sudden blindness).

  See *Invisibility*

Blood: (1) Angelic no-go zone (protection); (2) Harvesting angels (redeemed through the Blood); (3) Judgment (positive or negative)

(1) Exodus 12:23; (2) Matthew 13:41; Matthew 24:31; (3) Revelation 8:7-8; 16:3-4.

  See *Stop Sign*

Bodybuilder: (1) Strong angel (positive); (2) Strongman/hold (negative)

(1) 2 Thessalonians 1:7; 2 Peter 2:11; (2) Mark 5:2-9.

Border Control Agent: (1) Angelic protection; (2) Regional principality (fallen and elect)

(1) Genesis 3:24; Exodus 14:19-20; (2) Matthew 8:28; Mark 5:3-15; Daniel 10:5-20.

  See *Road Block* and *Stop Sign*

Bread: See *Food Bank, Manna,* and *Pizza*

Breaker angel: (1) Angel of breakthrough

(1) Genesis 24:40 (Hebrew "prosper" = break forth).

Bugle/r: See *Trumpet*

Butterfly: (1) Glorious angel

(1) Luke 2:9; Revelation 18:1
  See *Insect (winged)*

C

Car/s: (1-2) Angelic chariot

(1) 2 Kings 2:11; (Psalm 68:17 and Judges 13:20 [flames on side]); (2) Ezekiel 1:13 (as in "Where are your wheels?"); Acts 7:30.
  See *Chariots of Fire*

Caseworker: (1) Angel on personal assignment

(1) Daniel 10:11.
  See *Adjustment Bureau*

Caterer: (1) Angel delivering food

(1) 1 Kings 19:5-6

Chariots of Fire: (1) Angel host/ Army of heaven

(1) 2 Kings 6:17; 2 Kings 2:11.
  See *Cars*

Cherubim: (1) Covering angel; (2) Guard/Protector

(1-2) Exodus 25:18-20; Hebrews 9:5

Choir: Heavenly choir

(1) Psalm 148:2; Luke 2:13-14.
  See *Worship/per/s*

Cleaner: (1) Holy angel (separating from the world)

(1) Isaiah 6:6-7

Cloud: (1) Angel clothing; (2) Cloud shapes may represent angelic beings; (3) Heavenly vehicle

(1) Revelation 10:1; (3) Acts 1:9.
  See *Glory* and *Glory Cloud*

Coal/s: (1) Angel on purifying assignment

(1) Isaiah 6:6-7.
  See *Fire*

Cockatoo/s (white parrot): (1) Heavenly host/beings (birds repeating song); (2) Worshipping angels.

(1-2) Isaiah 6:3; Revelation 4:8.

See *Birds* and *Parrot (TDC)*

Coincidence (so called): (1) Angel/s have gone before you

(1) Genesis 24;7,14-15 (people could say the servant's meeting Rebekah was coincidence/luck)

Combine Harvester: See *Harvest/er*

Cook/Chef: (1) Angel preparing food

(1) 1 Kings 19:5-7

Counselor: (1) Angel releasing wisdom

(1) Zechariah 1:9ff;
  See *Instructor*

Courier: (1) Angelic message bearer

(1) Daniel 10:11-12; Luke 1:19, 26-31.
  See *Delivery Man, Dispatch Rider*, and *Messenger*

Courier Pigeon: See *Courier*

Court Attendant/Guard: (1) Throne room angel; (2) Angel awaiting an assignment

(1) 1 Peter 3:22; Revelation 7:11
  See *Guard*

Corner/s: (1) Angels at the four corners of the world

(1) Revelation 7:1 (person/s standing in corner/s).
  See *Court Attendant*

Crystal: (1) Heaven's purity and holiness.

(1) Ezekiel 1:22

Curtain: (1) Heavenly veil

(1) Exodus 26:31-33; Psalm 104:2; Isaiah 40:22

D

Dark/ness: (1) Veiled heavenly activity (without fear); (2) Evil spirit (with fear)

(1) Exodus 14:19-20 (dark cloud); Psalm 18:11; Psalm 97:2; (2) Job 30:26; Psalm 88:6; Psalm 91:6; Psalm 143:3; Isaiah 5:2.
  See *Cloud* and *Border Control Agent*

Deliverer: (1) Angelic courier; (2) Delivering angel

(1-2) Numbers 20:15-16; Psalm 34:7; Daniel 3:28; Luke 2:10; Acts 5:19; 12:7-10.
  See *Pizza*

Delivery Man: See *Courier* and *Deliverer*

Deliverance: (1) Deliverance angel

(1) Psalm 34:7; Psalm 91:11; Acts 12:8

THE DIVINITY CODE TO UNDERSTANDING ANGELS

Demolition Crew: (1) Angels bringing judgment; (2) Angels breaking stronghold of the enemy

(1-2) (Joshua 5:14; 6:20).

Destroyer: (1) Death angel (Spirit of death?)

(1) Exodus 12:23

Diplomat: (1) Angel mediating between heaven and earth

(1) Genesis 19:1; Acts 1:10-11; Revelation 1:1

Directions: (1) Angel arranging divine connections; (2) Four-faced spirit beings (facing different directions)

(1) Acts 8:26 (someone giving directions); (2) Ezekiel 1:10 (North, South, East, West)

See *Corners*

Dispatch Rider: (1) Angelic message bearer

(1) Ecclesiastes 5:6 (KJV).

See *Mailman*

Doctor: (1) Healing angel (MASH doctor); (2) Delivering angel (birthing)

(1) John 5:3-4; Matthew 8:8-9 (2) Judges 13:3,5

See *Midwife*

Dogfight (Aerial): (1) Angelic spiritual warfare

(1) Daniel 10:13,20; Ephesians 6:12; Revelation 12:7.

See *Marching*

Door: See *Portal*

Doorpost/s Shaking: (1) Voice of Angels; (2) Breakthrough / Deliverance

(1) Isaiah 6:3-4; John 12:29; (2) Acts 16:26 (unseen angelic activity)

Dolphin/s: (1) Can be symbolic of prophetic angels where their flippers and fins are as wings operating in a different environment (lives in water and sensitive to frequencies)

(1) Luke 2:13-14 (Pod); Revelation 10:5,8 (dolphins stand on their tails)

Doppelganger (Your Double): (1) Angel that is assigned and may look like a person

(1) Acts 12:15

Double (a person's look-alike): See *Doppelganger*

Dragonfly: (1) (+) Strengthening angel; (2) (-) Demonic powers; (3) Culturally may represent happiness (in Asia)

(1) Matthew 4:11 (also consider dragonflies eat mosquitos; (2) Revelation 9:7

E

Eagle: (1) Prophetic / revelatory angel; (2) All-seeing heavenly creature

(1) Isaiah 40:31; Ezekiel 1:10; (2) Revelation 4:7-8
  See *White Eagle* and entries in the *Divinity Code* book

Earthquake: (1) Resurrection angel; (2) The announcement of angelic presence; (3) Stirring / displacing a territorial spirit; (4) Angelic response to intercession; (5) Heavenly visitation; (6) Heavenly sign; (7) Host of heaven arriving; (8) Earth witnessing to a heavenly declaration; (9) Message from heaven arriving

(1-2) Matthew 28:2; (3) 1 Samuel 14:15; (4) Revelation 8:4-5; (5) Isaiah 29:6 (KJV); (6) Amos 1:1; (7) Zechariah 14:5; (8) Matthew 27:54; (9) Psalm 77:18; 97:4.

Emma: (1) Whole or Universal. Someone's personal encounter

Escape Artist: (1) Angel of deliverance

(1) Acts 12:15
  See *Stuntman*

Eunuch (gender neutral person): (1) Heavenly angel

(1) Matthew 22:30

Eyes (multiple): All-seeing spirit being; (2) Multidimensional spiritual sight; (3) Seer angels

(1-2) Ezekiel 1:18; Revelation 4:6; (3) Daniel 4:17.
  See *Lookout*

F

Farm Workers: (1) Harvest angels

(1) Ruth 2:15-16 (if Boaz is a type of Christ, his workers would be angels); Matthew 13:39; Revelation 14:15-19
  See *Harvest/er/s*

Feather/s: (1) Affirmation of the presence of angels; (2) Rising feathers may indicate ascension and vice versa

(1) Isaiah 6:2; (2) Genesis 28:12 (rising/falling);
  See *Wings*

FedEx: See *Parcel Delivery*

Fighter Jet: See *Airforce*

Fire: (1) Purifying angel; (2) Holy angel

(1) Exodus 3:2; (2) Isaiah 6:2-7; Hebrews 1
  See *Coal, Flame/s,* and *Pillar of Fire*

Food Bank Workers: (1) Angel supplying strength; (2) Angelic distribution

(1) Psalm 78:25
  See *Caterer*

Flame/s: (1) Purifying angel

(1) Judges 13:20; Ezekiel 1:13; Hebrews 1:7
  See *Fire*

Flames on Vehicle: (1) Angelic chariot

(1) 2 Kings 2:11; Psalm 104:4

Funeral Parlor Attendant: (1) Angelic escort (protecting / guarding)

(1) John 20:12
  See *Undertaker*

Furnace Worker: (1) Angel with you through a trial; (2) Winnowing angel

(1) Daniel 3:25,28; (2) Matthew 13:41-42

G

Gabriel: (1) "God is my Strong Man" (2) Archangel: (3) Messenger revealing the plans of God; (4) Releases understanding;

(2-4) Daniel 8:16; 9:21; Luke 1:19; 26

Gas Station: See *Mechanic* and *Pit Stop*

Gemstones: (1) Angel distributing gifts

(1) Ephesians 4:8
  See *Beryl, Crystal, Sapphire*

General: See *Officer (Armed Forces)*

Glory: (1) Angel from the Presence of God; (2) Glory angel/s

(1-2) Luke 2:9; Revelation 18:1

  See *Amber, Cloud,* and *Rainbow*

Glory Cloud: See *Cloud*

Golden Angel: (1) Angel of finance; (2) Angel of Ephesus (golden candlesticks); (3) Angel of Intercession (carrying golden censer); (4) Angel from God's presence

(1) Malachi 3:10-12 (hosts = angels); (2) Revelation 2:1-7; (3) Revelation 8:2-5; (4) Daniel 10:5

  See *Glory, Amber,* and *Rainbow*

Guard: (1) Guardian angel

(1) Matthew 18:10; Psalm 34:7; Psalm 91:11

Guide: (1) Angel providing direction

(1) Numbers 20:16; Matthew 28:5-6; Acts 8:26; 12:8

Griffin: (1) Heavenly winged-creature with eagle head and lion body

Daniel 7:4

Grim Reaper: (1) Spirit of Death

(1) Exodus 12:23 (NLT)

  See *Angel of Death, Plague, Spirit of Death, Suicide Bomber* and *Undertaker*

H

Harvest/er/s: (1) Harvest angel/s

(1) Matthew 13:39; Revelation 14:14-19.

  See *Farm Workers*

Hawk: (1) Good: Angel destroying poverty spirit (hawks hunt pigeon/s [=poverty spirit]); (2) Bad: Principality (preying on Christians)

(1) Malachi 3:11 [note: "Lord of hosts"] and Leviticus 5:7, Luke 2:24; (2) Psalm 102:7-8; Lamentations 3:52

See *Pigeon* in *Divinity Code*

Height: (1) Powerful angel (power relates to size of angel; larger = more power)

(1) Revelation 10:1,5

Highway Patrol: See *Policemen* and *Traffic Co*p

Homeland Security: See *Border Control*

Homeless Person: (1) God testing your heart through an angel

(1) Hebrews 13:2; (Be aware this could also be Jesus [Matthew 8:20])

Hydrotherapy: (1) Healing angel

(1) John 5:3-4 (in stirring waters)

I

Imaginary Friend: (1) Guardian angel

(1) (Matthew 18:10 and Daniel 10:7)

Immortal Person/s: (1) Angel/s. (2) Cloud of witnesses

(1) Luke 20:36; (2) Hebrews 12:1

Insect (winged): See *Ladybug*

Incense: (1) Angel carrying prayers to heaven; (2) Prayer portal

(1-2) Luke 1:11; Revelation 8:3

Insect (flying): See *Butterfly, Ladybug* and *Locust*

Instructor: (1) Angel of revelation

(1) Zechariah 1:9, 19; 4:4-5, 12-14; 6:4-5

  See *Counselor*

Interpreter (language): (1) Revelatory angel (decoding mysteries)

(1) 1 Corinthians 13:1 (Someone who can translate between languages)

Invisibility: See *Blinded* and *Transparency*

J

Jasper: (1) Treasurer (delivery of treasure)

(1) Tradition holds that one of the three magi was named Casper (same as Jasper)

Jegudiel: (1) Praise of God

(1) Psalm 148:2

Josiah: (1) Healing angel

(1) Meaning Yahweh heals

K

Kamikaze Pilot: See *Suicide Bomber*

Kokabiel: (1) Star of God; (2) Spirit of lust

(1) 1 Enoch 6:7-8; (2) Genesis 6:1-4

L

Ladder: See *Stairs*

Ladybug: (1) Guardian angel (protects fruit by killing aphids)

(1) Daniel 6:22

  See *Insect*

Lamp stand: (1) Angel bringing deliverance; (2) Angel bearing light (to a church)

(1) Acts 12:7; (2) Revelation 1:20.

Lawyer: (1) Angel referencing the law/Scripture

(1) Acts 7:53

Librarian: (1) Angel of scrolls/books (2) Angel releasing scrolls

(1-2) Revelation 10:1-2,8-9

Lightning: (1) Angels carrying God's Word; (2) God's arrows; (3) Revelatory angel/s; (4) Angel releasing power; (5) (-) Fallen angel

(1) 2 Samuel 22:14-15; Psalm 18:14; (2) Psalm 144:6; (3-4) Ezekiel 1:13-14; Daniel 10:6; Matthew 28:3; Revelation 4:5; (5) Luke 10:18; 2 Corinthians 11:14

Lion: (1) Spiritual authority

(1) Ezekiel 1:10

Lion Tamer: (1) Angel shutting the mouths of spiritual accusation/ authority

(1) Daniel 6:22

Locksmith: (1) Delivering angel

(1) Acts 12:7; Revelation 20:1

Locust/s: (1) Destroying spirits; (2) Abaddon/Apollyon (spirit from bottomless pit); (3) Spirit of death; (4) Financial destruction; (5) Judgment

(1) Revelation 9:3-10; (2) Revelation 9:11 (King of Locusts); (3) Exodus 10:4; 14:29

See *Angel of Death* and *Plague*

Lookout: (1) Protective/guardian angel; (2) Watcher angel/s

(1) Matthew 18:10; (2) Daniel 4:13, 23; Ezekiel 1:18; 10:12

   See *Eyes*

Lord of Hosts: (1) Jesus as Commander of Heaven's angelic armies

(1) 2 Kings 22:19; Luke 2:13

Loud Person: (1) Angel making decree; (2) Angel of judgment

(1) Daniel 10:6 (Voice of a multitude); (2) Revelation 14:9

Luck: See *Coincidence*

M

Mailman: (1) Angelic courier/messenger

(1) Luke 1:19.

   See *Dispatch Rider*

Manna: (1) Delivery from revelatory angel/s

(1) Deuteronomy 8:3 (manna = revelation) and Psalm 78:25

Marching: (1) Lord's host/Army of Heaven

(1) 2 Samuel 5:24; Matthew 26:53

   See *Army*

Marquee: (Elevated Sign): See *Sign/Sign Writer*

Mechanic: (1) Angel preparing your way

(1) Genesis 23:20

   See *Pit Stop* and *Wheel Technician*

Medic: (1) Healing angel

(1) 1 Kings 19:5; Daniel 10:19; Matthew 4:11; Matthew 8:9; Luke 22:43; John 5:4

Men in Black/Grey Suits
  See *Adjustment Bureau*

Men (in dreams or visions): (1) Angel/s
(1) Judges 13:16; Matthew 1:20; 2:19; Hebrews 13:2 (unknown person)

Messenger: (1) Revelatory angel
(1) 2 Kings 1:3; Luke 1:19; Revelation 1:1
  See *Courier*

Measuring Tape: (1) Angel on an assessment assignment
(1) Zechariah 2:1-3; Revelation 11:1.
  See *Tailor*

Michael: (1) Name meaning: 'Who is like God'; (2) Archangel; (3) Warring angel; (4) Healing angel
(2-3) Daniel 10:13, 21; Jude 1:9; Revelation 12:7; (4) Seen as a healing angel for some believers

Midwife: (1) Delivering angel; (2) Strengthening angel
(1) Judges 13:3; Luke 1:13, 31; (2) Luke 22:43; Hebrews 11:11

Mocker: (1) Evil spirit
(1) Acts 16:17-18

N

Nanny: (1) Guardian angel
(1) Matthew 18:10

Ninja: (1) Angelic special forces
(1) Joel 2:9,11.
  See *Stuntman*

O

Obstruction (difficulty along the way): (1) Guarding angel; (2) Angel opposing a wrong decision/path

(1) Genesis 3:24; (2) Numbers 22:22-34; Exodus 14:24
  See *Opposition*

Officer (Armed Forces): (1) Archangel

(1) Matthew 8:9 (commanding a chain of command); Jude 1:9
  See *Lord of Hosts*

Oil: (1) God imparting an anointing via the heavenly host

(1) 1 Samuel 16:13 (person in a dream anointing you could be an angel); Zechariah 4:2-6 (Someone pouring out oil); Isaiah 61:1

One-Time Encounter: (Meet someone and not meet them again)
  See *Stranger*

Opposition (removed): (1) Angelic advanced guard

(1) Exodus 33:2 (opposition cleared)
  See *Obstruction*

Orb (wheel within a wheel): (1) Revelatory angel

(1) Ezekiel 1:16

Optician: (1) Angel removing the veil

(1) 2 Kings 6:17

P

Paramedic: See *Medic*

Paratrooper: See *Ninja*

Parcel Delivery: (1) Revelatory angel
(1) Daniel 10: 5-8, 11-12,14; Revelation 10:10

Physiotherapist: (1) Healing angel

(1) John 5:3-4

  See *Hydrotherapist*

Pillar of Fire: (1) Angel of His glory; (2) Angel before His face

(1-2) (Exodus 14:19 and Exodus 13:21); Exodus 14:24

  See *Fire*

Pit Stop: (angel/s ministering): (1) Refreshing/Refueling in the Holy Spirit

(1) Genesis 24:46; 1 Kings 19:7-8; Matthew 4:11

  See *Mechanic* and *Wheel Technician*

Pizza: (1) Angelic Delivery; (2) Angel of revelation (solid food = revelation)

(1-2) Psalm 78:25; John 6:31; Luke 1:30-31; Revelation 10:10

  See *Deliverer, Mailman* and *Manna*

Plant Nurseryman: (1) Angelic midwife (spiritually we are trees: Psalm 1:3)

(1) Luke 1:31; Genesis 18:2,10-14; Hebrews 11:11 (Seed planters)

Plague (sickness): (1) Angel of destruction

(1) Exodus 12:23 (NLT); 2 Kings 19:35

  See *Locust/s*

Policeman/woman: (1) Angel of authority (protecting/directing); (2) Angel enforcing the law; (3) Corrupt cop/s

(1) Matthew 13:41; Genesis 3:24; (2) Hebrews 2:2; (3) Galatians 1:8.

  See *Prison Guard* and *Traffic Cop*

Pool Attendant: (1) Healing angel

(1) John 5:4 (stirring of the waters)

Portal: (1) Angelic Gateway/Stairway

(1) Genesis 28:12; John 1:51; Exodus 25:22; 30;6; 33:9, and Hebrews 8:5

Postman: See *Mailman*

Presence: (1) Spirit being (negative feeling); (2) Angel of God's glory (feeling of awe)

(1) Job 4:15-16; (2) Isaiah 6:2; (2 Thessalonians 1:9, Luke 1:19 [Isaiah 63:9])

  See *Presence of God*

Prison Guard: (1) Delivering angel; (2) Angelic key-holder

(1) Acts 5:19-20; (2) Revelation 9:1-2

  See *Policeman/woman*

Protection: (1) Guardian angel; (2) Angelic army escort

(1) Psalm 34:7; 91:10-11; (2) Genesis 32:1-3 (having been protected in a dangerous situation)

R

Raguel: (1) Defender of Justice

(1) Psalm 82:3

Raphael: (1) "God heals." Someone's personal encounter

(1) John 5:4

Rainbow: (1) Angel of glory

(1) Ezekiel 1:28; Revelation 10:1

  See *Amber* and *Glory*

Realtor (Real Estate Agent): (1) Angel securing property/land for the work of God

(1) 1 Chronicles 21:20-26 (Compare: 2 Samuel 24:18-25)

Remashel: (1) Evening of God; (2) Spirit of lust

(1) 1 Enoch 6:7-8; (2) Genesis 6:1-4

Revelator (someone releasing revelation): (1) Revelatory angel

(1) Luke 1:30-31; Revelation 1:1

  See *Courier* and *Delivery Man*

Roadblock: (1) Angel prohibiting entry

(1) Genesis 3:24

  See *Alcohol Testing* and *Stop Sign*

Road Workers: (1) Angels preparing the way; (2) Angels slowing the enemies progress

(1) Genesis 32:1; Exodus 23:20; Psalm 91:11-12; Acts 8:26; (2) Psalm 35:6

Room Service: (1) Revelatory angel; (2) Strengthening angel

(1) Psalm 78:25; (2) 1 Kings 19:5-8; Matthew 4:11

  See *Waiter*

S

SAS (special forces): See *Ninja*

Scorpions: (1) Spirits inflicting pain

(1) Revelation 9:1-4

Scroll: See *Librarian*

Seal (of Authority): (1) Decreeing angel

(1) Revelation 7:2

Seal (animal): (1) Revelatory angel (bearing a ball); (2) Decreeing angel (riding a wave)

(1) Ezekiel 1:16; (2) Revelation 7:2

Security Guard: See *Guard*

Seismologist: See *Earthquake*

Shemihazah: (1) My name has seen; (2) Spirit of lust.
(1) 1 Enoch 6:7-8; (2) Genesis 6:1-4

Shouting: See *Loud Person*

Sickle: (1) Harvest angel; (2) Spirit of death (with fear)
(1) Revelation 14:14-19; (2) Exodus 12: 23
  See *Grim Reaper* and *Harvest/er*

Sign/ Sign writer (prophetic sign): (1-2) Directive angel
(1) 1 Chronicles 21:16 (elevated sign); (2) Matthew 2:1-2, 9; Luke 2:10-12.
  See *Skywriter* and *Stop Sign*

Size (of angel): See *Height*

Skywriter: (1) Revelatory angel
(1) 1 Chronicles 21:16 (between heaven and earth, where the sword is a word)
  See *Sign/Sign writer*

Selaphiel: (1) Prayer of God
(1) Daniel 10:12

Septimus: (1) Seventh (Latin); (2) Angel of Rest
(1) Someone's personal encounter

Seraphim: (1) Six-winged angel
(1) Isaiah 6:6

Soldier: (1) Angel from the heavenly host; (2) Angel undertaking spiritual warfare

(1) Matthew 8:9; (2) Daniel 10:12-13

  See *Army*

Someone distributing prizes: (1) Angel carrying reward/s

(1) Matthew 16:27

Song/s: (1) Worshipping angels

(1) Hebrews 1:6

  See *Wake-Up Call*

Spirit of Death: (1) Exodus 12:23

  See *Angel of Death* and *Grim Reaper*

Stadium Crowd: (1) Innumerable angels; (2) Cloud of Witnesses

(1) Hebrews 12:22 (2) Hebrews 12:1

Stairs: (1) Angelic gateway; (2) Portal to Heaven

(1) Genesis 28:12 (people/angels ascending and/or descending)

Stars: (1) Angels of Heaven; (2) Angel of the seven churches

(1) Job 38:7; (2) Revelation 1:20

Steps: See *Stairs*

Stop Sign: (1) Angel prohibiting progress

(1) Genesis 3:24; Exodus 12:23; Luke 16:26 (spiritual barrier); Acts 16:7; Revelation 19:10; 22:8-9

  See *Road Block*

Stranger: (1) Angels undercover (angels unawares)

(1) Hebrews 13:2; Judges 6:11-17 (like on park bench); Judges 13:21 (one-time appearance)

Stuntman/Stunt Double: (1) God's specialist forces
(1) Joel 2:9, 11; Acts 12:15 (like an actor's double)
   See *Ninja*

Suit (person wearing suit and hat): See *Adjustment Bureau*

Suicide: See *Spirit of Death*

Suicide Bomber: (1) Spirit of Death
(1) John 13:27 and Matthew 27:5

Surveyor: See *Measuring Tape*

Sword: (1) Angel carrying the judgment/word of God
(1) Genesis 3:24; 1 Chronicles 21:16; and Hebrews 4:12

T

Tailor: (1) Angel sent to clothe you for a particular role
(1) Zechariah 3:5.
   See *Measuring Tape*

Teacher: See *Instructor*

Telescope: See *Binocular*

Throne/room (Beings around it): (1) Seraphim
(1) Isaiah 6:1ff

Thunder: (1) Voice of an angel
(1) John 12:29

Tour Guide: See *Guide*

Trades Person with Tape/Ruler: See *Measuring Tape*

Traffic Cop: (1) Harvest angel (cops screening people); (2) Guiding angel

(1) Matthew 13:49; (2) Acts 8:26
   See *Alcohol Testing* and *Policeman/woman*

Translator: See *Interpreter (language)*

***Tree (person under a tree)*:** (1) Angelic encounter

(1) Judges 6:11,19.
   See *Stranger*

Transparent Person: (1) Spirit being (good or evil)

(1) Job 4:15; Daniel 10:5-7
   See *Invisibility*

Trumpet / Player: (1) Herald angel; (2) Angel of declaration

(1) Matthew 24:31; Revelation 8:2; 8:6-11:15

U

***Unable to connect with a person/group*:** (1) Intervening angel

(1) Exodus 14:19-20
   See *Adjustment Bureau* and *Obstruction*

Undertaker (with peace): (1) Escort angel (taking someone home)

(1) Luke 16:22; 2 Kings 19:35; See *Angel of Death* and *Funeral Parlor Attendant*

Uriel: (1) Protector of Truth

(1) Personal encounter; Daniel 10:5-21

Usher: (1) Angelic guidance

(1) Exodus 32:34; Luke 16:22 (ushered into the Glory); Acts 12:10

USPS: See *Parcel Delivery*

W

Wake-Up Call: (1) Wakey wakey angel; (2) Your angel singing to you

(1) Zechariah 4:1; (2) Jeremiah 33:3 (waking to songs in your heart)

Waiter: (1) Angelic server (2) Angel bringing you into communion

(1) 1 Kings 19:5-8; Matthew 4:11; (2) 1 Kings 19:5

Watchman: (1) Watcher angel

(1) Ezekiel 1:18; Daniel 4:13,23

Waterfall (heaven's outpouring): (1) Angelic portal; (2) Heavenly outpouring; (3) Open heaven; (4) Financial blessing

(1) Ezekiel 1:24; (2-3) (Genesis 7:11 and John 1:51); (3-4) Malachi 3:10 (note: "Lord of hosts" means angels involved)

Weight Lifter: See *Body Builder*

Wheel Technician: (1) Angel bringing alignment

(1) Ezekiel 1:15; 10:9, 16; 11:22.
   See *Car, Chariot of Fire, Mechanic, Pit Stop,* and *Orb*

White: (1) Holy angel (person or angel clothed in white)

(1) Mark 16:5

White Eagle: (1) Prophetic angel; (2) Angel declaring righteousness

(1) Acts 1:10-11; (2) Revelation 16:5
   See *Eagle*

White Owl: (1) Angel that works with prophets in the wilderness

(1) John 1:23

Wind: (1) Winnowing angel

(1) Psalm 35:5 (someone driven away by strong wind)

Wings: (1) Angelic shelter/covering/protection; (2) Angelic activity/location/service; (3) Worship; (4) Heavenly beings

(1) Psalm 91; (2)Exodus 37:9; Hebrews 8:5; 1 Kings 6:24,27; Isaiah 6:2; Ezekiel 1:11, 23; 10:8, 16; (3) Isaiah 6: 2; (4) Ezekiel 1:6-11.
   See *Feather/s*

Wisdom (to discern): (1) Angel of wisdom

(1) 2 Samuel 14:17,20

Witness/es: (1) Angels or saints watching on as witnesses

(1)Genesis 18:21; 1 Timothy 5:21; Hebrews 12:1
   See *Lookout*

Woman/Women: (1) Angel
   See *Men*

Worship/per/s: (1) Heavenly choir

(1) Luke 2:13-14; Revelation 5:11-12; 7:11
   See *Choir*

Wrestler: (1) Angel resisting you to bring a revelation

(1) Hosea 12:3-4

Z

Zookeeper: (1) Gathering angel

(1) Genesis 6:20 (who gathered the animals?); Daniel 6:22; (Matthew 24:31 and Acts 10:11-28 [the vision of animals is a commission to go to the four corners of the earth to gather souls])

ABOUT THE AUTHORS

Adam F. Thompson has a remarkable grace to interpret dreams, release words of knowledge, and operate in the prophetic. Supernatural signs and manifestations regularly accompany his ministry as he desires to see Jesus magnified through the moving of the Holy Spirit. He has ministered extensively in Pakistan, India, Africa, Indonesia, Papua New Guinea, Malaysia, and the Philippines in crusades, feeding programs, and pastor conferences. He is coauthor of *The Divinity Code* and author of *The Supernatural Man* and *Living from Heaven*. Adam operates itinerantly through his ministry Voice of Fire: www.voiceoffireministries.org.

Adrian Beale is an itinerant prophetic revelator who imparts the spirits of wisdom and understanding (Isaiah 11:2). His ability in Scripture to see beyond the surface narratives to reveal eternal truths is exceptional. He is coauthor of *The Divinity Code,* author of *Mystic Awakening,* and loves to interpret dreams publicly and release people into Kingdom realities.

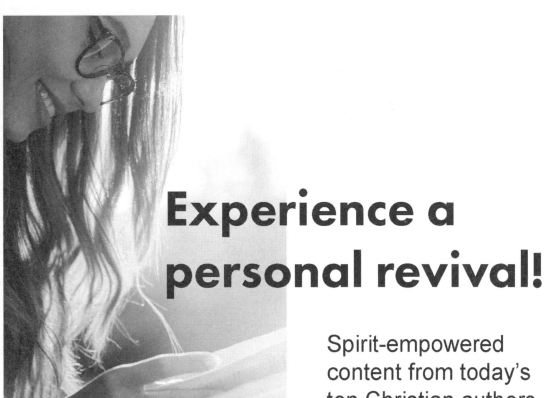